CASTLES OF
OF
·SAND·

Grateful acknowledgment is made to the following publishers, authors, and agents for their permission to reprint copyrighted material. Any adaptations are noted in the individual acknowledgments and are made with the full knowledge and approval of the authors or their representatives. Every effort has been made to locate all copyright proprietors; any errors or omissions in copyright notice are inadvertent and will be corrected in future printings as they are discovered.

Alexander and the Terrible, Horrible, No Good, Very Bad Day by Judith Viorst and illustrated by Ray Cruz. Text copyright © 1972 by Judith Viorst. Pictures copyright © 1972 by Ray Cruz. Reprinted by permission of the American publisher, Macmillan Publishing Company, of the British publisher, Angus & Robertson (UK), and of the author's agents, Lescher & Lescher, Ltd.

"The Boy Who Cried Wolf" adapted by Genie Iverson, © 1989 by Genie Iverson.

"A Day When Frogs Wear Shoes" adapted from *More Stories Julian Tells* by Ann Cameron, illustrated by Ann Strugnell. Copyright © 1986 by Ann Cameron. Illustrations copyright © 1986 by Ann Strugnell. Reprinted by permission of the American publisher, Alfred A. Knopf, Inc., and of the British publisher, Victor Gollancz Ltd.

Forecast by Malcolm Hall, illustrated by Bruce Degen. Text copyright © 1977 by Malcolm Hall, illustrations © 1977 by Bruce Degen. Adapted and reprinted by permission of Coward, McCann & Geoghegan.

"General Store" from *Taxis and Toadstools* by Rachel Field. Copyright 1926 by Rachel Field. Reprinted by permission of the American publisher, Doubleday, a division of Bantam, Doubleday, Dell Publishing Group, Inc., and of the British publisher, William Heinemann Ltd.

Acknowledgments continue on pages 382–384, which constitute an extension of this copyright page.

WORLD OF READING

CASTLES OF SAND

P. David Pearson   Dale D. Johnson

Theodore Clymer   Roselmina Indrisano   Richard L. Venezky

James F. Baumann   Elfrieda Hiebert   Marian Toth

Consulting Authors

Carl Grant   Jeanne Paratore

SILVER BURDETT & GINN

NEEDHAM, MA • MORRISTOWN, NJ
ATLANTA, GA • CINCINNATI, OH • DALLAS, TX
MENLO PARK, CA • DEERFIELD, IL

A WATERY WORLD

UNIT TWO

UNIT
TWO

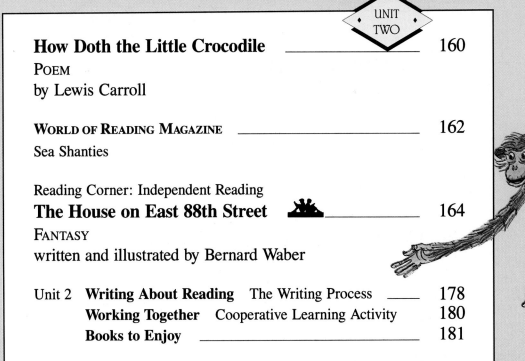

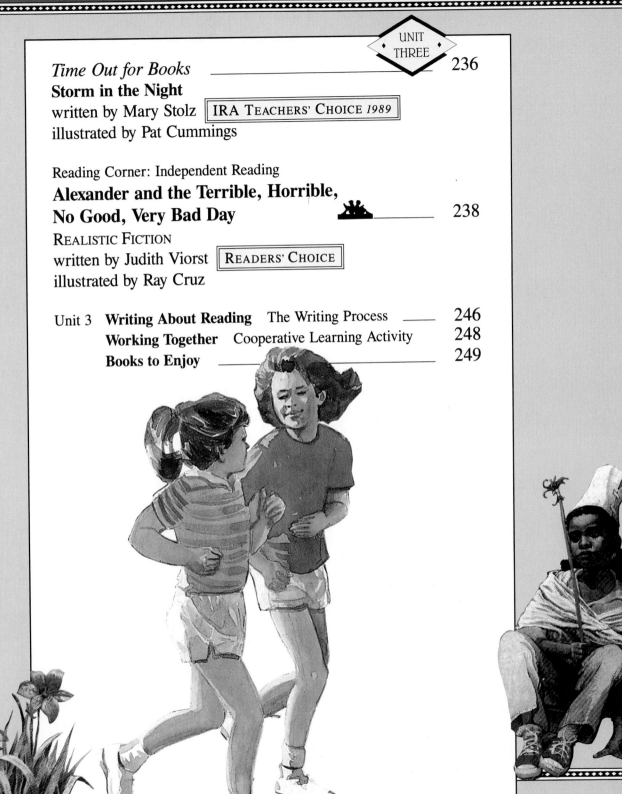

UNIT
THREE

Get the Message

REMEMBER WHEN...

*R*eading can help us learn about the past.

What events from the past are worth remembering?

detail of SNAP THE WHIP, *oil on canvas by Winslow Homer, American, 1872*

When I Was Nine

written and illustrated by James Stevenson

The author of this story tells about a special time when he was about your age.

My own children are grown up now; that's how old I am. But sometimes I look back and I remember. . . .

When I was nine, we lived on a street with big trees.

I had a bicycle, and I knew where all the bumps were on the sidewalk.

We had a dog named Jocko.

Our telephone looked like this.
Our number was 3348.

My father had boots and a
bugle from when he was in the
army in the First World War, and a mandolin
from when he was in school. Sometimes
when he came home from work, he would
play taps for us.

At night our mother would read to us.

We lived near a railroad. Before I went to sleep, I listened to the steam locomotives. The freight trains and the express trains blew their whistles as they went racketing by in the dark.

In our backyard there was a beech tree. If you climbed high enough, you could see the Hudson River and smoke from the trains.

After school I listened to the radio and did homework. (There was no television.)

Bill, who lived next door, was my best friend. He was ten. Bill was pretty good fun, but only about half the time.

When my brother had a friend over, they wouldn't let me play. I learned to pitch by throwing a ball against the garage door.

I skated on a pond in the winter. The ice would crack with a tremendous booming noise. But everybody said not to worry.

I put out a weekly newspaper. I collected news from all the people on our block.

DID ANYTHING HAPPEN THIS WEEK?

No.

HOW I PRINTED <u>THE</u> <u>NEIGHBORHOOD</u> <u>NEWS</u>

① I TOOK A CAN OF HEKTOGRAPH AND OPENED IT. HEKTOGRAPH WAS LIKE A THICK JELLY SOUP.

② I DUMPED IT INTO A SAUCEPAN AND HEATED IT ON THE STOVE,

③ THEN POURED IT INTO A PAN AND LET IT COOL AND HARDEN.

④ MEANWHILE, I WROTE THE PAPER WITH A SPECIAL PURPLE PENCIL.

⑤ THEN I PUT THAT PAPER FACE-DOWN ON THE HARD JELLY AND RUBBED IT SMOOTH.

⑥ WHEN I PULLED OFF THE PAPER---

(7.) ---THE NEIGHBORHOOD NEWS WAS WRITTEN ON THE JELLY BACKWARDS!

(8.) THEN I PUT A CLEAN SHEET OF PAPER ON IT AND RUBBED, AND I GOT A COPY OF THE NEWS. I COULD MAKE LOTS OF COPIES.

Not everybody wanted one.

MR. FINERTY, WOULD YOU LIKE TO BUY A COPY OF THE NEIGHBORHOOD NEWS?

NOT RIGHT NOW.

Most summers my brother and I went to visit our grandmother, who had a house near the beach. We went swimming every day.

Grandma was a lot of fun. We would crawl into her room in the morning and hide under her bed.

Then we would pretend to be a funny radio program; she always acted surprised and she always laughed.

But this summer was different. In July we packed up the car for a trip out west. A neighbor said he would take care of Jocko. Bill and Tony waved goodbye.

We drove for days and days. My brother and
I argued a lot. When it got too bad, our father
stopped the car and made us throw a football for
a while. Then we got back in the car again.

At the end of each day we looked for a
place to stay. "What do we think?" my father
would say.

"Plenty good enough," my mother would
say. And we would stop for the night.

My brother and I always wanted to stop and
see something special. Our parents usually
wanted to keep going. "Too touristy," they said.
But in Missouri we visited a big cave.

Our parents woke us up one night to look at
the sky. "What's happening?" I asked. The sky
was shimmering.

"It's the Northern Lights," said my mother.

On my birthday we stopped in a small town and went into a store. My parents bought me exactly what I always wanted . . . a cowboy hat.

At last we came to New Mexico.

We stayed at a ranch and went on long, hot rides into the mountains.

One day we rode to a waterfall. While the horses rested, we slid down the waterfall and plunged into an icy pool. We did it again and again.

It was the most fun I'd ever had.

We drove back home in August. As we turned into our block, Jocko ran to greet us. It was great to get home.

Everything looked just the way it always had . . . except maybe a little smaller.

But I was probably a little bigger. I wasn't nine any more.

◆ LIBRARY LINK ◆

If you liked this story by James Stevenson, you might enjoy reading another of his books, Howard.

Reader's Response

Do you think you would have liked the trip to New Mexico as much as the author did? Why or why not?

When I Was Nine

Thinking It Over

1. Why wasn't there a television set in the author's house?
2. How did the summer when the author was nine compare to other summers?
3. What were some of the sights the family saw on the way to New Mexico?
4. How can you tell that the author liked his grandmother?
5. Was the author happy when he was a boy? How do you know?

Writing to Learn

THINK AND PREDICT   Mr. Stevenson writes about a special year of his childhood. When you are grown up, what do you think you will remember about this year of your life? Read Mr. Stevenson's list. Then write your own list.

Things Mr. Stevenson Remembered	Things I Will Remember About This Year
• Dad had a bugle. • Mother read to us. • I put out a newspaper.	(Make your list.)

WRITE   Read your list. Circle your favorite memory. Write sentences to tell what you will remember about this year when you grow up.

General Store

Some day I'm going to have a store
With a tinkly bell hung over the door,
With real glass cases and counters wide
And drawers all spilly with things inside.
There'll be a little of everything;
Bolts of calico; balls of string;
Jars of peppermint; tins of tea;
Pots and kettles and crockery;
Seeds in packets; scissors bright;
Kegs of sugar, brown and white;
Sarsaparilla for picnic lunches,
Bananas and rubber boots in bunches.
I'll fix the window and dust each shelf,
And take the money in all myself,
It will be my store and I will say:
"What can I do for you to-day?"

Rachel Field

Making a Comparison Chart

How can you better understand the characters you read about? One good way is to make a comparison chart.

Learning the Strategy

As you read, you learn some of the details of a character's life. You may learn what a character eats, and how he or she dresses and talks. The author uses these details to help you understand the world a character lives in. If you list details about the character's life, you can compare them with your own life. A comparison chart is one way to help you understand how a character's life and your life are the same and different.

Read the paragraph below and then look at the comparison chart that follows. Compare things that Karen has done with things you may have done.

> Karen put on her shawl and walked to town. Her high-button shoes kept sinking in the mud. She went into the candle maker's shop and bought candles. Then she walked to the miller's. Her freshly ground bag of flour was waiting for her.

COMPARISON CHART

Where Karen went and what she did	I have done this.	I have not done this.
wore high-button shoes		✓
went to the candle maker		✓
bought candles	✓	
bought flour	✓	

A comparison chart may help you better understand how Karen's life and yours are the same and different.

Using the Strategy

Copy and fill out the chart below for "When I Was Nine." Then compare the things the author has done with the things you have done.

COMPARISON CHART

Where the boy went and what he did.	I have done this.	I have not done this.
traveled west		
listened to a radio		
learned to pitch		
saw the northern lights		

Applying the Strategy to the Next Story

As you read the next story, "Thy Friend, Obadiah," compare Obadiah's life with your life. Then you can make a comparison chart.

The writing connection can be found on page 45.

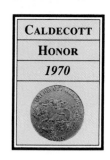

If you had an unusual friend like Obadiah's, you might feel and act just the way he did!

Thy Friend, Obadiah

written and illustrated by Brinton Turkle

Wherever Obadiah went, a sea gull was following him. It followed him all the way to the candle maker's, and it was waiting for him when he came out of the shop.

When he was sent to the wharf for a fresh codfish, it hopped along behind him.

And at night when he went to bed, he could see it from his window. There it was, perched on the chimney of the shed, facing into the wind. Of all the sea gulls on Nantucket Island, why did this one go everywhere Obadiah went?

On First Day, everyone dressed up warmly and went to Meeting. The Starbuck family formed a little parade. First, Father and Mother. Then Moses and Asa and Rebecca and Obadiah and Rachel. Behind them came the sea gull, hopping along as if it were going to Meeting too.

"Go away!" said Obadiah. The bird fluttered off, but it soon came back.

"Thee has a friend, Obadiah," said Father as he turned in at the Meeting House gate.

"Obadiah has a friend!" said Moses.

"Obadiah has a friend!" said Rebecca.

"Ask thy friend to come into Meeting," said Asa.

Rachel didn't tease. She tried to take Obadiah's hand; but he didn't want to hold anybody's hand. He picked up a pebble and threw it at the bird. He missed. The sea gull flew out of sight, but when Meeting was over, there it was—waiting for him.

It got so that Obadiah didn't want to go out of his house.

At breakfast, Father said, "Obadiah, how is thy friend?"

"What friend?" asked Obadiah, his mouth full of muffin and plum jam.

"Thy very own sea gull!" said Asa.

Rebecca giggled.

"That bird is *not* my friend!" Obadiah shouted.

Mother raised a finger. "Don't distress thyself, Obadiah," she said. "I think it is very nice that one of God's creatures favors thee."

"Well, *I* don't like it," said Obadiah. "Sea gulls don't follow anyone else around!"

Soon after breakfast it began to snow. In the afternoon, Mother wrapped a woolen scarf around Obadiah and sent him to Jacob Slade's mill with some money and a sack for flour. ◄◆►

Have you ever gone to a mill to buy flour?

The bird was nowhere to be seen. "Maybe it doesn't like the snow," Obadiah told himself. "Maybe it flew away to the mainland." He was so glad it wasn't hopping along after him that he made duck tracks all the way up Jacob Slade's hill.

The miller filled the flour sack, and Obadiah gave him the money Mother had tucked in his mitten.

"Keep this, lad," Jacob Slade said, giving him a penny. "And don't let it burn a hole in thy pocket."

On the way home, Obadiah tried to slide on a patch of ice, but he skidded and fell head over heels. His hat went flying. Snow got in his ears and in his boots. His breeches got wet and so did the sack of flour. His knee hurt and the penny was gone forever in the snowbank. He was all alone on the hill. Shivering and sniffling, he picked himself up and limped home.

Sea gulls were perched on almost every housetop on Orange Street; but he couldn't find the special sea gull that had been following him. The birds were faced into the raw east wind and paid no attention to him at all.

Mother was very cross about the wet flour. She gave Obadiah a hot bath and dry clothes and right after supper she made him drink something hot that tasted awful. "Is thy knee still hurting thee?" she asked. ◄❖►

◄❖►
What do you do when you come home wet and cold?

"It's better." Obadiah wished he felt better about the lost penny.

"Then get into bed."

Obadiah said his prayers, and as soon as Mother was gone, he got out of bed and tiptoed to the window. The sea gull was not there. He got back into bed again and wondered what had happened.

32

The next day and the next day and the day after that,
no bird followed Obadiah when he left his house. Every
night he looked out of his window, but the sea gull didn't
come back.

Then he saw it down at the wharf. It was with some
other gulls where a little fishing boat was docked; but
something was wrong. A large rusty fishhook dangled from
its beak.

"That's what happens when thee steals from a fishing
line. Serves thee right," Obadiah said and walked away.

He was on the cobblestone street by the blacksmith's shop when he discovered that the sea gull was hopping along behind him.

Obadiah stopped. The bird stopped. The fishhook bobbed in the wind.

"If thee is quiet, I'll try to get that off thy beak."

The sea gull didn't move.

"I won't hurt thee," Obadiah said.

The bird allowed him to come nearer and nearer. In a moment, the fishhook was in Obadiah's hand, and the sea gull was wheeling into the sky making little mewing sounds. It flew out toward the lighthouse. Obadiah watched until he couldn't see it any longer; then he threw the rusty hook away and went home.

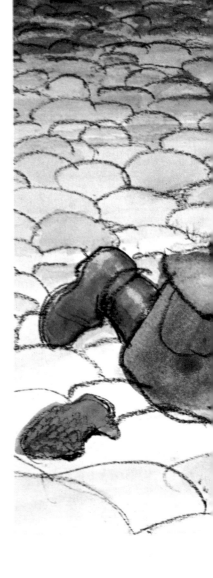

As soon as he opened the front door, Obadiah smelled bread baking. In the kitchen, Mother and Rachel were just taking it out of the oven. Mother cut him a slice of the fresh, warm bread and spread it with butter. He sat on a stool to eat it and between mouthfuls he told them what had happened. ❖❖❖

"Well," said Rachel, "thee won't see that silly old bird again."

"No," said Obadiah. "I expect I won't."

❖❖❖
Have you ever smelled freshly baked bread?

At bedtime, after she had tucked him in, Mother went
to the window. "Obadiah," she said. "Look here."

He tumbled out of bed.

"Isn't that thy sea gull?"

There it was on the chimney, facing into the wind in
the clear blue night!

"That's him!" said Obadiah. "He looks cold out
there, Mother."

"His feathers keep him warm. But thee doesn't have feathers, Obadiah. Get back into bed quickly before thee takes a chill."

Obadiah jumped into bed again and Mother kissed him good night.

The wind whistled around the corner of the house and Obadiah snuggled down into the quilts.

"Mother. . . ."

"Yes, Obadiah."

"That sea gull *is* my friend."

"I'm glad, Obadiah. Good night."

"And Mother. . . ."

Mother turned at the door. Her candle flickered and almost went out. "Yes, Obadiah," she said.

"Since I helped him, I'm *his* friend, too."

Make a comparison chart. List things Obadiah did. Check the things you have done. Check the things you have *not* done.

◆ LIBRARY LINK ◆

If you enjoyed this story by Brinton Turkle, you might like to read his other books, such as Obadiah, the Bold *and* The Fiddler of High Lonesome.

Reader's Response

Do you think an animal can really be your friend? Tell why.

Thy Friend, Obadiah

Thinking It Over

1. Why was Obadiah so annoyed at the beginning of the story?
2. Why did Obadiah try to send the bird away?
3. When did Obadiah first begin to miss the sea gull?
4. How did Obadiah feel about the bird before he helped it? How did he feel afterward?
5. Suppose Obadiah had not helped the bird. What might have happened? How did you decide on your answer?

Writing to Learn

THINK AND CONNECT Obadiah learns something about helping others. It is written in the "thought link" below.

Because I helped the sea gull, / the sea gull is my friend.

Finish another "thought link."

If I help someone,

WRITE You discovered something about helping others when you finished your "thought link." Write some sentences to tell what may happen if you help someone.

Imagine leaving your home and moving to a new land across the ocean. A group of brave people made such a trip more than three hundred years ago.

Life in Pilgrim Times

by Carlotta Dunn

About 370 years ago, a group of people left their homes in England to come to a place they had never seen before. For two long months their ship, the *Mayflower,* sailed across the wide and stormy Atlantic Ocean. Finally, on November 9, 1620, they landed on the rocky shores of North America and settled in a place they called Plymouth, named after the city in England from which they had sailed.

Who were these brave people, and why did they leave their homes in England? This small group of brave families were the Pilgrims. A pilgrim is a person who makes a journey for religious reasons. These people were called Pilgrims because they left their homes to find a place where they would be free to follow their religious beliefs.

In 1620, the Pilgrims arrived on the *Mayflower*.

The Pilgrims Work to Build a New Life

After the Pilgrims arrived in North America, they had only the things they brought with them on the ship. They had clothes, weapons, some tools and books, and a few pieces of furniture. Their food was almost gone, so they had to hunt or fish. Luckily, the forests of North America were full of animals, nuts, and berries, and the ocean was rich in fish.

The Pilgrims had to clear the land to build homes.

Still, life was very difficult for the Pilgrims. They had to chop down trees to get wood to build homes. The first houses the Pilgrims built were small and simple. The roofs were made of grasses mixed with mud, and the walls were made of wood. Most houses had only one large room with a large fireplace that provided the only heat for the family in the winter. The family cooked, ate, played, worked, and read together in that room.

After the Pilgrims built homes, they cut down trees to clear the land for farms. Most of the Pilgrims had come from cities in England, so they knew little about farming. If they were to survive, they would need help.

The Pilgrims Get Help from New Friends

Luckily for the Pilgrims, help came to them about four months after they landed in North America. One day, an Indian named Samoset walked into Plymouth, and to the surprise of the Pilgrims, Samoset spoke English. He had learned the language from English sailors who had come to fish in North America. The Pilgrims didn't know it at the time, but Samoset would help them build a new life in their new land.

Indians watch as the Pilgrims land at Plymouth.

Samoset brought an Indian named Squanto to Plymouth. Squanto spoke even better English than Samoset. Together, Squanto and Samoset taught the Pilgrims many things that helped them during their first year in North America. The Indians taught the Pilgrims how to farm and gave them corn to plant. Corn was new to the Pilgrims, for the people in England knew nothing about this crop. The Indians showed the Pilgrims where the best places to fish and hunt were. They took the Pilgrims into the forests and showed them which fruits and berries were safe to eat, and which ones would hurt them. The Pilgrims thanked God for their good fortune in finding such wonderful friends.

The Pilgrims share the harvest with their Indian friends.

The Pilgrims learned to read using horn books like this one.

The Pilgrims Believe in God and Education

God was never far from the minds and hearts of the Pilgrims. After all, they had come to North America so they could worship God in their own way. As soon as they were able to, the Pilgrims built a meetinghouse where they came together on Sunday to pray. Everyone in Plymouth attended services at the meetinghouse, and everyone followed the rules set down by the ministers, their religious leaders. It was the Pilgrims' strong beliefs that gave them the strength to build a new life.

The second most important part of Pilgrim life was education. The Pilgrims wanted their children to learn to read so that they would be able to read the Bible. They built the first English schools in North America.

Pilgrim Families Work Together

Religion and education were not the only important parts of Pilgrim life. The family was also very important. Fathers taught their sons how to hunt, farm, fish, build tools and toys, and many other things. Mothers taught their daughters how to cook, sew, farm, and to care for younger children in the family. There was plenty of work for everyone, and the family had to work together to make sure that they had all the things they needed.

Everyone in the family was loved and cared for. Mothers and fathers liked to watch their children play games, and they liked to read to them and tell them stories from the Bible. Life may have been hard for the Pilgrims, but the love they shared and their strong religious beliefs more than made up for the hard times.

◆ LIBRARY LINK ◆

If you would like to learn more about the pilgrims, you might enjoy The Plymouth Thanksgiving *by Leonard Weisgard.*

 Reader's Response

What is it about the Pilgrims that you most admire?

Life in Pilgrim Times

Thinking It Over

1. How do you think the Pilgrims felt when they landed in North America?
2. What were some of the ways in which the Indians showed their friendship?
3. Why did the Pilgrims know so little about living off the land? How do you know?
4. Do you think the Pilgrims would have survived without the help of the Indians? Why or why not?
5. Name three of the Pilgrims' strongest beliefs.

Writing to Learn

THINK AND COMPARE Have you ever done any of the things the Pilgrims did? Compare your life with theirs. Complete the comparison chart below. Add more things the Pilgrims did. Then check the things you have done and the things you have never done.

What the Pilgrims did	I have done	I have not done
ate corn	✓	
ate fish		
built houses		

WRITE Write a paragraph to explain how your life is like the Pilgrims' lives or how it is different.

Reading Social Studies

You have been reading about daily life in America's past. Maps from long ago can also tell you about the past. An old map can show what your community was like one hundred years ago.

Today, maps are an important part of everyday life. We read maps when we travel or when we want to see where someone lives. We also read them when we study about people and places.

To read maps you need some special skills. These special skills include:

♦ Using a *map key*. A map key explains the colors and symbols that are used in a map.

♦ Using a *scale*. A scale is a numbered line that helps you find the distance between places.

♦ Using a *compass rose*. A compass rose is a drawing that shows where north, south, east, and west are on a map.

Learning how to use the map key, the scale, and the compass rose will help you read and understand maps.

How to Read a Map

You can use this map of California to practice using the map key, scale, and the compass rose.

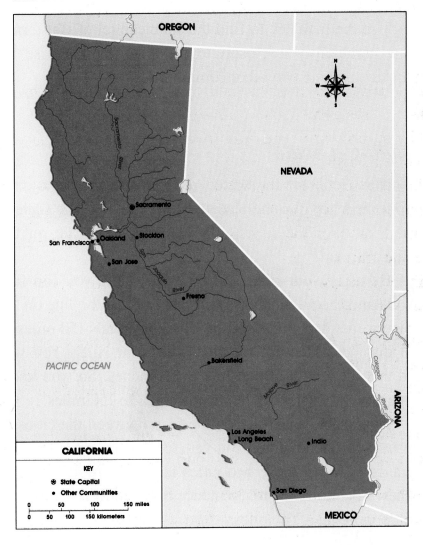

47

Reading a Map Key

First, learn what information a map can tell by looking at the map key. Map keys use symbols and colors to stand for real places. On the map of California, the key is in the bottom left corner. This map key has two symbols. One symbol shows the state capital. The other symbol shows other communities.

Use the map key to find the state capital of California. What community is closest to the state capital? Use the map key to name two other communities.

Reading a Scale

Next, look for the scale. You can use the scale on a map to find how far one place is from another. The scale is usually part of the map key. Where is the scale on the California map?

By using your ruler and the map scale, you can find the distance between any two places. Look at the line on the scale for the map of California. The line equals 150 miles of real distance. Measure the line with your ruler. You will find that the length of that line is $1^1/_4$ inches. So, you know that every $1^1/_4$ inches on the map is equal to 150 miles.

Now place your ruler on the map between the cities of Fresno and Sacramento. You can see on the ruler that the distance between these two cities is a little more than $1^1/_4$ inches. Therefore, the real distance between the two cities is a little more than 150 miles.

Look again at the scale. Notice that it gives distances in miles and kilometers. Map scales often show distance in both miles and kilometers.

Reading a Compass Rose

A compass rose is a special drawing that shows directions on the map. Now look for the compass rose on the map of California. You will find it in the top right corner.

The words *north*, *south*, *east*, and *west* name directions. The letters *N*, *S*, *E*, and *W* on the compass rose stand for these words. The line on the compass rose labeled *N* points in the direction of the earth's North Pole. The line labeled *S* points in the direction of the South Pole. The line labeled *E* is on the right of the rose, and the line labeled *W* is on the left. The in-between directions are northeast, southeast, southwest, and northwest. These are shown on the compass rose by the letters *NE, SE, SW,* and *NW.*

The compass rose helps you find places on maps. Look again at the map of California. Suppose someone asked you which direction to travel to go from San Jose to Bakersfield. You could answer by using the map and compass rose. Lay a ruler on a line from San Jose to Bakersfield. Notice that the ruler lies in the same direction as the line in the compass rose labeled *SE*. So, the person would need to travel southeast to go from San Jose to Bakersfield.

As You Read Read the following pages from a social studies book. Then answer the questions on page 55.

3 Studying One Community

Learning Through Maps

How do maps help you learn about your community?

VOCABULARY

port   county

Let's Learn About Our Community We all live in communities. Each of us may think that our community is the most important one. The truth is that every community is important. Every community has its own special people and places.

The city of Wilmington, North Carolina, is located on the Cape Fear River. Wilmington was settled in 1732.
■ Why, do you think, was this location for a city a good one?

We cannot learn about all of our communities. Instead we will visit a class in one community. The students in this class will tell us how they learned about their community. We can use many of these same ways to study our own community.

We will visit a class of girls and boys who go to Forest Hills Elementary School. The school is in Wilmington, North Carolina.

A Good Way to Begin   The students told their teacher, Mrs. Reddrick, that they wanted to learn more about their community. Mrs. Reddrick asked them what they already knew about Wilmington. The students discovered that they really knew a lot. They knew that Wilmington is a **port** city. A port is a place where ships can be safe from the big waves and strong winds of stormy seas. The boys and girls knew that many ships come to their city's port every year.

Mrs. Reddrick then asked the students to tell her what they wanted to study. This helped her to group the class so that students with the same interests could work together.

Now we will look at each group to see how they studied their community and what they learned.

Learning from Maps   Antonio, Tonya, Ben, and Kelsey had moved to Wilmington during the summer. They wanted to make maps. These maps would help them find places in their new community. They decided to make four maps. Mrs. Reddrick gave them some maps to

(Left) Mrs. Reddrick helps her class learn about their city and state. (Right) Kelsey, a student in Mrs. Reddrick's class, points to the location of Wilmington.
▪ What tells you that this class is studying about North Carolina?

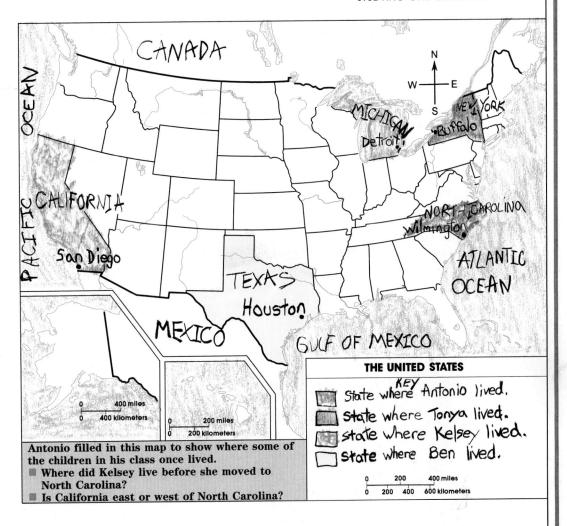

THE UNITED STATES

KEY
State where Antonio lived.
State where Tonya lived.
State where Kelsey lived.
State where Ben lived.

Antonio filled in this map to show where some of the children in his class once lived.
■ Where did Kelsey live before she moved to North Carolina?
■ Is California east or west of North Carolina?

use. These maps showed the outlines of certain places. The maps also showed a compass rose and a scale of miles. The girls and boys filled in the maps and made map keys.

Antonio filled in a map of the United States. He colored North Carolina red and put a black dot where Wilmington is located. Antonio also colored the states where he, Tonya, Ben, and Kelsey used to live. He put black dots where their old communities are located. Then he filled in the names of all these places. Look at Antonio's map above. Where did he live before moving to Wilmington?

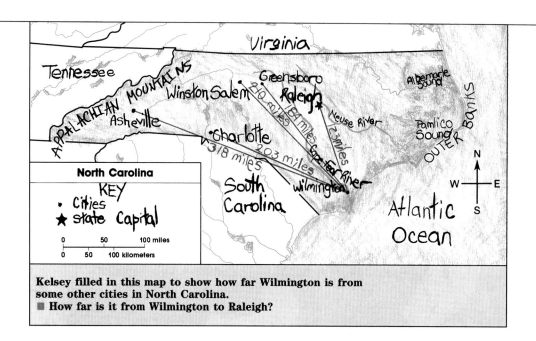

Kelsey filled in this map to show how far Wilmington is from some other cities in North Carolina.
■ How far is it from Wilmington to Raleigh?

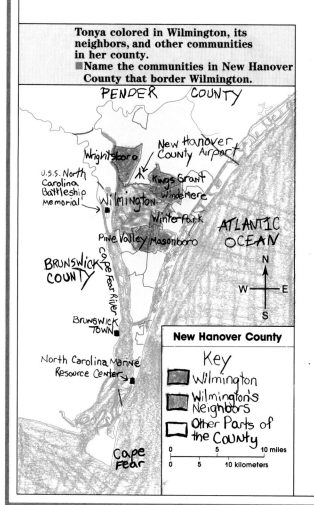

Tonya colored in Wilmington, its neighbors, and other communities in her county.
■ Name the communities in New Hanover County that border Wilmington.

Kelsey wanted to make a map of North Carolina. She located Wilmington on her map. She also showed other cities in the state and how far they are from Wilmington. Kelsey drew in the Appalachian Mountains, the Cape Fear River, the Neuse River, Albemarle Sound, Pamlico Sound, and the Outer Banks.

Tonya's map shows the **county** named New Hanover County. A county is a political division. Most of our states are divided into counties. Besides showing the shape of New Hanover County, Tonya's map shows some of the communities in the county.

Using What You Have Learned

Read the map on page 53 to answer the following questions.

1. What state did Ben live in before moving to Wilmington?

2. About how far apart are San Diego and Wilmington?

3. In what direction would you travel if you wanted to go from the state of New York to North Carolina?

Read the maps on page 54 to answer the following questions. In your answers, tell if you used the map key, the scale, or the compass rose to answer the question.

4. What color is used to show Wilmington on the New Hanover County map?

5. In New Hanover County, how far is Brunswick Town from Wilmington?

6. Look at the map of North Carolina. In what direction would you travel to go from Wilmington to Raleigh?

7. Which map would you use to find the state capital of North Carolina? Why would you use this map?

8. What city shown on the map of North Carolina is the farthest from Wilmington?

Examples and excerpts are from *Our Country's Communities, Silver Burdett & Ginn Social Studies,* © 1988.

Going to Grandaddy's place made Momma happy. But that's not the way Janetta felt.

Grandaddy's Place

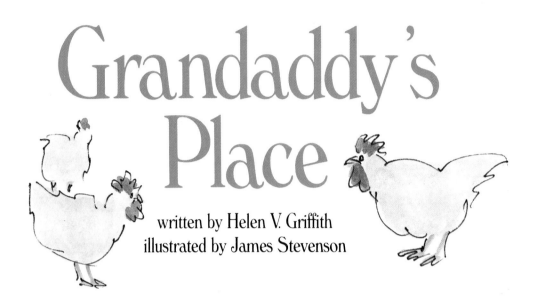

written by Helen V. Griffith
illustrated by James Stevenson

CHAPTER ONE

One day Momma said to Janetta, "It's time you knew your grandaddy." Momma and Janetta went to the railroad station and got on a train. Janetta had never ridden on a train before. It was a long ride, but she liked it. She liked hearing about Momma's growing-up days as they rode along. She didn't even mind sitting up all night.

But when they got to Grandaddy's place, Janetta didn't like it at all.

The house was old and small. The yard was mostly bare red dirt. There was a broken-down shed and a broken-down fence.

"I don't want to stay here," said Janetta.

Momma said, "This is where I grew up."

An old man came out onto the porch.

"Say hello to your grandaddy," Momma said.

Janetta was too shy to say hello.

"You hear me, Janetta?" Momma asked.

"Let her be," said Grandaddy.

So Momma just said, "Stay out here and play while I visit with your grandaddy."

They left Janetta standing on the porch. She
didn't know what to do. She had never been in
the country before. She thought she might sit on
the porch, but there was a mean-looking cat on
the only chair. She thought she might sit on the
steps, but there was a wasps' nest up under the
roof. The wasps looked meaner than the cat.
Some chickens were taking a dust-bath
in the yard. When Janetta came near,
they made mean sounds at her.

Janetta walked away. She watched the ground
for bugs and snakes. All at once a giant animal
came out of the broken-down shed. It came
straight toward Janetta, and it was moving fast.
Janetta turned and ran. She ran past the chickens
and the wasps' nest and the mean-looking cat.

She ran into the house.

"There's a giant animal out there," she said.

Grandaddy looked surprised. "First I knew of it," he said.

"It has long legs and long ears and a real long nose," said Janetta.

Momma laughed. "Sounds like the mule," she said.

"Could be," said Grandaddy. "That mule's a tall mule."

"It chased me," said Janetta.

"It won't hurt you," Momma said. "Go back outside and make friends." But Janetta wouldn't go back outside.

"Nothing out there likes me," she said.

CHAPTER TWO

After dark Momma and Grandaddy and Janetta sat out on the steps. The mean-looking cat wasn't anywhere around. Janetta hoped the wasps were asleep. She was beginning to feel sleepy herself. Then a terrible sound from the woods brought her wide awake.

"Was that the mule?" she asked.

"That was just an old hoot owl singing his song," said Grandaddy.

"It didn't sound like singing to me," said Janetta.

"If you were an owl, you'd be tapping your feet," said Grandaddy.

They sat and listened to the owl, and then Grandaddy said, "It was just this kind of night when the star fell into the yard."

"What star?" asked Janetta.

"Now, Daddy," said Momma.

"It's a fact," said Grandaddy. "It landed with a thump, and it looked all around, and it said, 'Where am I?'"

"You mean stars speak English?" asked Janetta.

"I guess they do," said Grandaddy, "because English is all I know, and I understood that star just fine."

"What did you say to the star?" asked Janetta.

Grandaddy said, "I told that star, 'You're in the United States of America,' and the star said, 'No, I mean what planet is this?' and I said, 'This is the planet Earth.'"

"Stop talking foolishness to that child," Momma said.

"What did the star say?" asked Janetta.

"The star said it didn't want to be on the planet Earth," said Grandaddy. "It said it wanted to get back up in the sky where it came from."

"So what did you do, Grandaddy?" Janetta asked.

"Nothing," said Grandaddy, "because just then the star saw my old mule."

"Was the star scared?" Janetta asked.

"Not a bit," said Grandaddy. "The star said, 'Can that mule jump?' and I said, 'Fair, for a mule,' and the star said, 'Good enough.' Then the star hopped up on the mule's back and said, 'Jump.'"

Momma said, "Now, you just stop that talk."

"Don't stop, Grandaddy," said Janetta.

"Well," Grandaddy said, "the mule jumped, and when they were high enough up, the star hopped off and the mule came back down again."

"Was the mule all right?" asked Janetta.

"It was thoughtful for a few days, that's all," said Grandaddy.

Janetta stared up at the sky. "Which star was it, Grandaddy?" she asked.

"Now, Janetta," Momma said, "you know that's a made-up story."

Grandaddy looked up at the stars. "I used to know," he said, "but I'm not sure anymore."

"I bet the mule remembers," Janetta said.

"It very likely does," said Grandaddy.

From somewhere in the bushes some cats began to yowl. "That's just the worst sound I know," Momma said. "Janetta, chase those cats."

"They're just singing their songs," said Grandaddy.

"That's right, Momma," said Janetta. "If you were a cat, you'd be tapping your feet."

Momma laughed and shook her head. "One of you is as bad as the other," she said.

CHAPTER THREE

The next day Grandaddy and Janetta went fishing. Janetta had never been fishing before. She didn't like it when Grandaddy put a worm on the hook.

"Doesn't that hurt him?" she asked.

"I'll ask him," said Grandaddy. He held the
worm up in front of his face. "Worm, how do you
feel about this hook?" he asked. He held the
worm up to his ear and listened. Then he said to
Janetta, "It's all right. That worm says there's
nothing he'd rather do than fish."

"I want to hear him say that," Janetta said.
She took the worm and held it up to her ear.
"He's not saying anything," she said.

"That worm is shy," said Grandaddy. "But I
know he just can't wait to go fishing."

Grandaddy threw the line into the water. It wasn't long before he caught a fish. Then he gave Janetta the pole so that she could try. She threw the line in, and before long she had a fish, too. It was just a little fish. Janetta looked at it lying on the bank. It was moving its fins and opening and closing its mouth.

"I think it's trying to talk," Janetta said.

"It may be, at that," said Grandaddy. He held the fish up to his ear. "It says, 'Cook me with plenty of cornmeal,'" said Grandaddy.

"I want to hear it say that," said Janetta.

"Can you understand fish-talk?" asked Grandaddy.

"I don't know," said Janetta.

"Well, all that fish can talk is fish-talk," said Grandaddy.

Janetta held the fish up to her ear and listened. "It says, 'Throw me back,'" Janetta said.

Grandaddy looked surprised. "Is that a fact?" he asked.

"Clear as anything," said Janetta.

"Well, then I guess you'd better throw it back," said Grandaddy.

Janetta dropped the little fish into the water and watched it swim away. Grandaddy threw the line back in and began to fish again. "I never saw anybody learn fish-talk so fast," he said.

"I'm going to learn worm-talk next," said Janetta.

CHAPTER FOUR

When they had enough fish for supper, Janetta and Grandaddy walked on home. The mean-looking cat came running to meet them. He purred loud purrs and rubbed against their legs.

"I didn't know that cat was friendly," Janetta said.

"He's friendly when you've been fishing," said Grandaddy.

The mule came out of the shed and walked toward them with its ears straight up. Janetta didn't know whether to run or not. The mule walked up to her and pushed her with its nose. Janetta was sorry she hadn't run.

"What do you know," Grandaddy said. "That old mule likes you."

"How can you tell?" Janetta asked.

"It only pushes you that way if it likes you," said Grandaddy.

"Really?" asked Janetta.

"It's a fact," said Grandaddy. "Up until now that mule has only pushed me and the cat and one of the chickens." Janetta was glad she hadn't run. She reached out her hand and touched the mule's nose.

"Grandaddy," she said, "What's the mule's name?"

"Never needed one," said Grandaddy. "It's the only mule around."

"Can I name it?" asked Janetta.

"You surely can," said Grandaddy.

Janetta thought. "I could call it Nosey," she said.

"That would suit that mule fine," said Grandaddy.

Janetta thought some more. "Maybe I'll call it Beauty," she said.

"That's a name I never would have thought of," said Grandaddy.

The mule gave Janetta another push. "This mule really likes me," Janetta said. "It must know I'm going to give it a name."

"You don't have to give it anything," said Grandaddy. "That mule just likes you for your own self."

〰〰 CHAPTER FIVE 〰〰

After supper Grandaddy and Momma and Janetta sat out on the steps and watched the night come on. The stars began to show themselves, one by one.

"Now I know what I'll name that mule," Janetta said. "I'll call it Star."

"Should have thought of that myself," said Grandaddy.

"Tomorrow I'll give the cat a name," said Janetta.

"Only fair, now the mule has one," said Grandaddy.

"After I get to know the chickens, I'll name them, too," said Janetta. "Then you'll be able to call them when you want them."

"That'll be handy," said Grandaddy.

"You'll be naming the hoot owl next," Momma said.

"I've been thinking about it," said Janetta.

Momma laughed, and Grandaddy did, too.

"Now, how did we get along around here before you came?" he asked.

"I've been wondering that, too, Grandaddy," said Janetta.

Reader's Response

Do you think you would like it at Grandaddy's place? Tell why or why not.

Grandaddy's Place

Thinking It Over

1. Why didn't Janetta like her grandaddy's place at first?
2. When did Janetta begin to like being there? How do you know?
3. How did Janetta's grandaddy make her feel less afraid?
4. Why did Janetta name the mule "Star"?
5. Suppose Janetta had stayed indoors because she was afraid. What might have happened?

Writing to Learn

THINK AND PREDICT When Janetta arrived at her grandaddy's place, she said, "Nothing out there likes me." What will she say when she leaves the farm? Draw a speech balloon.

Janetta

WRITE Fill the speech balloon with Janetta's words. Write what she might say when she leaves the farm.

Over the River and Through the Wood

Over the river, and through the wood,
  To grandfather's house we go;
    The horse knows the way
    To carry the sleigh,
  Through the white and drifted snow.

Over the river, and through the wood,
  To grandfather's house away!
    We would not stop
    For doll or top,
  For 'tis Thanksgiving Day.

70

Over the river, and through the wood—
  Oh, how the wind does blow!
    It stings the toes,
    And bites the nose,
  As over the ground we go.

Over the river, and through the wood,
  With a clear blue winter sky,
    The dogs do bark,
    And children hark,
  As we go jingling by.

Over the river, and through the wood—
  When grandmother sees us come,
    She will say, "Oh, dear,
    The children are here,
  Bring a pie for every one."

Over the river, and through the wood—
  Now grandmother's cap I spy!
    Hurrah for the fun!
    Is the pudding done?
  Hurrah for the pumpkin-pie!

Lydia Maria Child

The White Stallion

written by Elizabeth Shub
illustrated by Rachel Isadora

Imagine going on a trip with your family and meeting wild animals. This is what happens to Gretchen.

This is a true story, Gretchen. My grandmother Gretchen, your great-great-grandmother, told it to me. She was as young as you are when it happened. She was as old as I am when I heard it from her.

It was 1845. Three families were on their way West. They planned to settle there. They traveled in covered wagons. Each wagon was drawn by four horses. Conestoga wagons they were called.

Gretchen and her family were in the last wagon. Mother and Father sat on the driver's seat. The children were inside with the household goods.

Bedding, blankets, pots and pans, a table, chairs, a dresser took up most of the space. There was not much room left for Trudy, John, Billy, and Gretchen. Gretchen was the youngest.

Behind the wagon walked Anna, their old mare. She was not tied to the wagon but followed faithfully. She carried two sacks of corn meal on her back.

It was hot in the noonday sun. The children were cranky and bored. The wagon cover shaded them, but little air came in through the openings at front and back.

John kicked Billy. Billy pushed him, and he bumped Gretchen. Trudy, the oldest, who was trying to read, scolded them.

Their quarrel was interrupted by Father's voice. "Quick, everybody, look out! There's a herd of mustangs." The children clambered to the back of the wagon.

In the distance they could see the wild horses. The horses galloped swiftly and in minutes were out of sight.

"Look at Anna," John said. The old mare stood rigid. She had turned her head toward the mustangs. Her usually floppy ears were lifted high. The wagon had moved some distance before Anna trotted after it.

It was hotter than ever inside.

"Father," Gretchen called, "may I ride Anna for a while?"

Father stopped the wagon and came to the back. He lifted Gretchen onto the mare. The meal sacks made a comfortable seat. He tied her securely so that she would not fall off.

As they moved on, Gretchen fell asleep, lulled by the warmth of the sun. They were following a trail in Texas along the Guadalupe (gwäd ä $\overline{loo}'$ pe) River. The rear wheel of the first wagon hit a boulder, and the axle broke. The whole train stopped. Anna strayed away, with Gretchen sleeping on her back. No one noticed.

The travelers made camp. Children were sent for firewood and for water from the river. The women prepared food.

It was not until the axle had been fixed and they were ready to eat that Gretchen and Anna were missed.

The men tried to follow the mare's tracks but soon lost them. It was getting dark. There was nothing to do but remain where they were. They would search again at the first sign of light.

Faithful Anna, they thought, would return. She probably had discovered a rich patch of mesquite grass. She would come back when she had eaten all she wanted.

Gretchen awoke to the sound of lapping. Anna was drinking noisily from a stream. A short distance away stood a herd of ten or twelve wild horses. They were brownish in color. Some had darker stripes down their backs. Others had dark markings on their legs. They were mares.

After Anna had finished drinking, she moved toward them. And they walked forward as if to greet her. When they came close, they neighed and nickered.

They crossed necks with Anna, nuzzled her and rubbed against her. They were so friendly that Gretchen was not afraid. And she did not realize that Anna had wandered far from the wagon train.

Suddenly the horses began to nibble at the sacks on Anna's back. They had smelled the corn meal. In their eagerness they nipped Gretchen's legs. Gretchen screamed. She tried to move out of the way. She tried to loosen the ropes that tied her. But she could not reach the knots. Terrified, Gretchen screamed and screamed.

Out of nowhere a great white stallion appeared. He pranced and whinnied. He swished his long white tail. He stood on his hind legs, his white mane flying.

The mares moved quickly out of his way. The white stallion came up to Anna. He carefully bit through the ropes that tied Gretchen. Then, gently, he took hold of the back of her dress with his teeth. He lifted her to the ground.

77

He seemed to motion to the mares with his head, and then he galloped away. The mares followed at once. Anna followed them. Gretchen was left alone.

She did not know what to do. "Father will find me soon," she said out loud to comfort herself. She was hungry, but there was nothing to eat. She walked to the stream and drank some water. Then she sat down on a rock to wait.

She waited and waited, but there was no sign of Father. And no sign of Anna. Shadows began to fall. The sun went down. The dark came. "Anna!" Gretchen called. "Anna! Anna! Anna!"

There was no answering sound. She heard a coyote howl. She heard the rustling of leaves and the call of redbirds. Gretchen began to cry.

She made a place for herself on some dry leaves near a tree trunk. She curled up against it, and cried and cried until she fell asleep.

Morning light woke Gretchen. The stream sparkled in the sunlight. Gretchen washed her face and drank the clear water.

She looked for Anna. She called her name, but Anna did not come. Gretchen was so hungry she chewed some sweet grass. But it had a nasty taste, and she spat it out.

She sat on her rock near the stream. She looked at the red bite marks on her legs and began to cry again.

A squirrel came by. It looked at her in such a funny way that she stopped crying.

She walked along the stream. She knew she must not go far. "If you are lost," Mother had warned, "stay where you are. That will make it easier to find you." Gretchen walked back to her rock.

It was afternoon when she heard the sound of hooves. A moment later Anna ambled up to the stream. The sacks of meal were gone. The old mare drank greedily. Gretchen hugged and kissed her. She patted her back. Anna would find her way back to the wagon train.

She tried to climb on Anna's back, but even without the sacks the mare was too high. There was a fallen tree not far away. Gretchen wanted to use it as a step. She tugged at Anna, but Anna would not move. Gretchen pulled and shoved. She begged and pleaded. Anna stood firm.

Now again the white stallion appeared. Again he lifted Gretchen by the back of her dress. He sat her on Anna's back. He nuzzled and pushed the old mare. Anna began to walk. The white stallion walked close behind her for a few paces. Then, as if to say goodbye, he stood on his hind legs, whinnied, and galloped away.

Gretchen always believed the white stallion had told Anna to take her back to the wagon train. For that is what Anna did.

Your great-great grandmother Gretchen bore the scars of the wild mare bites for the rest of her life. I know because when she told me the story, she pulled down her stockings. And I saw them.

◆ LIBRARY LINK ◆

If you enjoyed this story, you might want to read The Girl Who Loved Wild Horses *by Paul Goble.*

Reader's Response

Gretchen was in danger when she became separated from her family. Do you think she acted wisely? Tell why or why not.

The White Stallion

Thinking It Over

1. Who is telling the story?
2. Where does the story take place?
3. Why do you think Gretchen asked to ride Anna?
4. How did Gretchen get back to her family?
5. Why did many of the pioneers travel together in wagon trains? What makes you think that?
6. Do you think this is a true story? Tell why or why not.

Writing to Learn

THINK AND RECALL Gretchen got lost as her family traveled to a new place. Can you remember an adventure you have had? Have you ever gotten lost, gone to a new place, or had some other interesting experience? When it happened, how did you feel? Copy and complete the chart below.

What Happened to Gretchen	How Gretchen Felt
Gretchen got lost.	Gretchen felt scared.
What Happened to Me	How I Felt
I _____.	I felt _____.

WRITE Write some sentences about an adventure you have had. Tell what happened and how you felt about it.

TIME OUT FOR

BOOKS

Lewis Carroll Shelf Award
ALA Notable Book
Best Books for Children

Hans Christian Andersen's
THE NIGHTINGALE

TRANSLATED BY *Eva Le Gallienne*

ILLUSTRATED BY NANCY EKHOLM BURKERT

Suddenly, through the window, came the sound of an exquisite song. It was the little, living Nightingale, perched on a branch outside. from *The Nightingale* by Hans Christian Andersen

Hans Christian Andersen was born almost two hundred years ago, but many of his stories are still favorites today. Some people think that "The Ugly Duckling," "The Emperor's New Clothes," and "The Princess and the Pea" are his best. These stories are so popular that you may have already read them, or maybe someone read them to you when you were younger.

When Mr. Andersen was a little boy, his father read to him a lot. His father also made Hans a toy theater so that Hans could write and act out his own plays and stories.

When Hans Christian Andersen grew up, he continued to write. He traveled and heard many tales and stories. Many of these stories he wrote down in his own words. He also wrote original stories like "The Little Mermaid," that he made up by himself. You can read *The Nightingale* to find out for yourself why Mr. Andersen and his stories are loved by readers even today.

If people can't read, how can they find their
way around? Long ago in Eagle's Landing, Mr.
Peaceable had the answer.

Mr. Peaceable PAINTS

written and illustrated
by Leonard Weisgard

Once, long ago, there was a little town growing up on a hill beside the sea. A town called Eagle's Landing. And when the wind blew in from the water, there was the smell of salt and fish. And when the wind blew from the west across the hill, there was the smell of farms and of wood smoke rising from the chimneys.

In Eagle's Landing, long, long ago, there were little lanes that led around the town and down to the sea, but there were no street signs, since some of the people didn't know how to read. And the houses were not numbered. But the townspeople always knew where they were, or where they wanted to be, by the pictures hanging above the tradesmen's shops.

And in those long ago times, there was always a night watchman. Mr. Dunstable was the night watchman in Eagle's Landing. All night long he marched up and down the little streets, with his lantern and his bell. It was his job to keep watch, to see that all was well.

Down a lane he walked, past the Sign of the Lamb. All was well at Mr. Pettibone's meat shop.

He walked across to the Sign of the Fish. All was well at Mr. Goodspeed's fish market.

And under the big maple tree, at the Sign of the Boot, all was well at the cobbler's, Mr. Adams.

Mr. Dunstable turned right at the Sign of the Clock. All seemed well at Mr. Peabody's clock and furniture shop.

At the Sign of the Cracker Barrel, Mr. Goodey Gates waved to Mr. Dunstable from inside his general store.

And at the sign with the shapes of the sun and the moon and stars, all was always well. For this was the shop of the painter and decorator of coaches and carriages. All the signboards in Eagle's Landing—all but one—were made here by Mr. Peaceable, the artist and sign painter.

"Six o'clock! And from the watch I am free. And now everyone may his own watchman be!" At sunrise every morning, when the steeple bells struck six, Mr. Dunstable bellowed this. Then his watch was over. He blew out his lantern, hung it from his staff, and, shouldering his stick, he marched on. His night's work was done.

Mr. Dunstable climbed up on the hill, past the little schoolhouse and crossed the village green towards home. When he came up to Mr. George Lion's Inn, all was not well there. Something was wrong! The Inn sign was gone! This was the only sign in town that wasn't a picture. It had lettering on it and everyone agreed it wasn't pretty—especially since it was hung upside down!

The innkeeper in Eagle's Landing was Mr.
George Lion. He was the jolliest man, and
certainly the roundest, but everyone in town
agreed he was also the stubbornest. George Lion
liked to say he was a poet. He enjoyed words and
loved to use them. So he made up rhymes. Once
a traveling painter had stopped at the Inn. In
exchange for food and lodging he had lettered
George Lion's favorite poem on a signboard for
the Inn.

But as Mr. George Lion could neither read nor write he had, by mistake, hung the sign upside down. Then who could possibly read it? But he stubbornly refused to put it right side up, so everyone, especially the children, called his tavern "Topsy Turvy Inn."

Just as Mr. George Lion was tying his apron around his middle, Mr. Dunstable came along.

"Ah, good morning to you, good Watchman Dunstable, what can I do for you?"

"A very good morning to you, Mr. Lion. I was just finishing off the watch, and on my way home. As a matter of fact, I was reciting your poem, which I know by heart:

Good cheer, good muffins and good tea
Dispatched with neatness and great dignity.
Coil up your ropes and anchor here
Till better weather does appear.
I've made my sign a little wider
To let you know I sell good cider!

"Well, I was thinking of a good cup of tea, when I looked up and saw your signboard gone! All could not be well, I thought."

"Heaven's to Betsy! MY SIGNBOARD GONE!" roared Mr. George Lion. "Six ships are sailing into the harbor this very morning. How will anybody ever know where to find my Inn? Where is my topsy turvy sign?"

Mr. George Lion rushed out, not even removing his apron, to search for his sign. Mr. Dunstable was just left standing there.

As the sun peered over the steeple that morning, six sailing vessels dropped anchor in the harbor of Eagle's Landing. The church bells began to ring.

Everyone came running. Farmers coming down from their farms to market, walked their sheep and cattle through the toll gate. They hurried through the little town to see the ships sail in. The children and their teacher declared that day a holiday. Even the tradesmen, excited as children, closed their shops. They all trundled down to see the ships come in. Sea captains' wives and sailors' families marched down to greet their men home from the seas. Everyone waved, everyone shouted and everyone watched.

The sailors tied the ships fast to the docks. The sails were folded and lashed safe to the masts. Then the sailors unloaded the ships, each with its cargo from some far-off land.

There was whale oil in the hold. There were barrels and boxes and chests and casks. Coffee beans in sacks. Sugar and tea and spices and rice. Silks and fans and ivory from the Orient. There were cats from Persia. Sleigh bells and iron work from Russia. Animal hides and gold dust from Africa.

And all this time Mr. George Lion was still searching everywhere for his topsy turvy sign.

Of course by now the little town was empty. Even the dogs and cats were down beside the sea, watching the boats unload. Everyone was there but Mr. Lion—and Mr. Peaceable.

Now anyone in Eagle's Landing could tell you right away who Mr. Peaceable was. He was a most happy man. Not just because he smiled and grinned a lot, and his eyes twinkled brightly. Not just because he sang or whistled while he worked. No, and not just because Mrs. Peaceable was very proud of him.

For from Mondays through Sundays, Mr. Peaceable, the artist and sign painter, did what he liked and liked what he did. He always said, "I like painting anything and everything under the sun and the moon and the stars!" And so if ever you were looking for Mr. Peaceable, at any time of the day or night, you could always find him painting in his shop.

Suddenly, without knocking, Mr. George Lion stormed through the sign painter's doorway.

"Mr. Peaceable! My signboard is gone!" raged Mr. Lion, "and the new stagecoach bringing in the mail is due any moment. The ships are already unloading in the harbor. Without my sign how will anybody ever be able to find my Inn? I can't letter a new one in time. It took a long time to make up the old sign. Heaven's to Betsy, but I am sunk!" And George Lion sank back into a chair. And just then he caught a glimpse of a painting that Mr. Peaceable was finishing.

"Mr. Peaceable, you do paint everything under the sun and the moon and the stars! What a handsome picture of a lion! He is not a wild lion, not an angry lion, not at all fearsome. He's almost a smiling lion! And Heaven's to Betsy! That lion does seem to resemble me!" Now Mr. George Lion began to look more like his old self.

"Good Mr. Peaceable, I would like to buy that lion! I will pay you well! Maybe with your picture of the lion they'll stop calling my tavern 'Topsy Turvy Inn'."

"The painting has already been sold, Mr. George Lion!" and Mr. Peaceable's eyes twinkled. "Your wife ordered this picture for you. Your sign is there in the corner. It fell down during the night. I was going to clean it up and bring them both over to you this very morning."

"Mr. Peaceable, I have an idea! Let's put
your lion and my poem together!" suggested
George Lion.

"What a wonderful signboard that will be!"
agreed Mr. Peaceable. And, before you could say
Eagle's Landing, the two men set the painting and
the sign together.

Together they secured an iron hinge to hold
it. Together they left the shop and hurried across
the village green to the Inn. And together they
hung the new signboard. But this time the
letters—not topsy turvy—were right side up.

And just in time too! For now the sailors
and the townspeople climbed up the hill to
the village green. And just at that very moment
the new mail coach rolled to a stop before the
crowd of people.

"Shiver my timbers!" shouted a sailor. "The topsy turvy sign's gone!"

"Great guns!" said the coach driver. "A new sign!"

Mr. Pettibone the butcher said, "Hen's teeth and cow's horns, if that lion isn't the image of George Lion! And such a peaceful lion!"

"A Peaceable Lion!" corrected Mr. Goodspeed, who always knew Mr. Peaceable's work when he saw it.

Everyone was very pleased.

But that was long ago. And yet today if ever you should happen to find yourself in Eagle's Landing you may know it at once. There are some new signs but some of the old ones still remain. And if you climb up the hill from the sea and cross the village green you may still see an old Inn with a signboard swinging out front—an Inn which is known for miles around as the Inn of the Peaceable Lion.

Reader's Response

Did you think Mr. Peaceable had a good idea for George Lion's sign? Why? What kind of sign might you have painted for the Inn?

WRITING
—ABOUT—
READING

Writing About Something
that Happened to You

The stories in this unit tell about events that people like to remember. For example, "When I Was Nine" describes a family trip to New Mexico. What exciting or fun things have happened to you? Think of an event to write about in a paragraph.

Prewriting

Think of a time that you like to remember. Copy the chart below onto your paper. Fill it in with information about the event.

The Time I _____	
What Happened?	
Who Was There?	
When?	
How Did I Feel?	

Writing

Use the information in your chart to write a paragraph about the personal experience you chose. Put in enough information so that your readers know exactly what you are writing about. Tell the events in the order in which they happened.

Revising

Have someone else listen while you read your paragraph. Ask, ''What part of my story do you want to know more about?'' Add details that answer your partner's questions. Think of a title for your paragraph.

Proofreading

Check to see if you indented the first word in your paragraph. Make sure you put a period or a question mark at the end of each sentence.

Publishing

Make a magazine of everyone's stories. You might call the magazine *Remember When*.

WORKING TOGETHER

Talking About the Past

In this unit you read about people who lived in America at different times and in different places. Now your group will "Remember When," and discuss what it might have been like to live in one of the story settings.

Here are some jobs you can do as you work together.

◆ Help others recall the stories in the unit.

◆ Ask questions to get people talking.

◆ Encourage others to share ideas.

◆ Agree or disagree in a nice way.

Begin by remembering some of the stories in this unit. Talk about where and when they took place. Agree on one setting to talk about.

As a group, think about what it might have been like to live in that place and time. Talk about questions such as: "What would your day be like?" "What would you like best about living then?" "What would be hard?" You might want to write a few words on paper to help the group remember all the ideas.

As a group, agree on one thing that would be the most different from life today and one thing that would be the same.

And Then What Happened, Paul Revere? by Jean Fritz *(Putnam, 1973)* This is a funny account of Paul Revere's famous ride to alert the Americans that the British were coming.

The Bears on Hemlock Mountain by Alice Dalgliesh *(Scribner, 1952)* Jonathan believes bears *really* live on Hemlock Mountain. Then his mother sends him to borrow a kettle from an aunt who lives on the other side of the mountain!

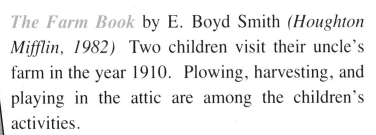

The Farm Book by E. Boyd Smith *(Houghton Mifflin, 1982)* Two children visit their uncle's farm in the year 1910. Plowing, harvesting, and playing in the attic are among the children's activities.

Wagon Wheels by Barbara Brenner *(Harper & Row, 1984)* This story is based upon the true account of the Muldies, a black family who left the South after the Civil War to settle in the West.

A WATERY WORLD

*M*any tales have been told about the seven seas.

What adventures await us in these watery worlds?

FISH IN WATER,
*Contemporary Chinese Watercolor
On Silk*

Tim had always wanted to be a sailor. One happy day, he got his wish. He found that life at sea was full of adventure and exciting challenges.

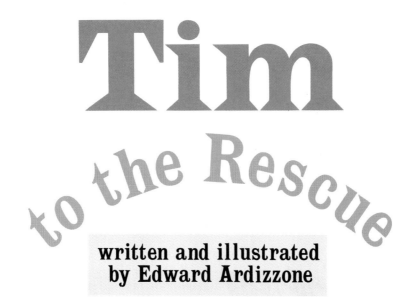

Tim to the Rescue

written and illustrated by Edward Ardizzone

Little Tim was in his house by the sea. It was stormy weather, and Tim was looking out the window and wishing that he were on some ship tossing about among the waves. But Tim had promised his parents to stay at home and work hard, and a promise like this has to be kept.

"Oh, dear," said Tim to himself. "I am bored with my sums, but I suppose I must learn them if I am to become a real sailor."

Suddenly there was a knock at the door. It was Tim's good friend Captain McFee, the old sea captain. Tim longed to go to sea with the captain, and he begged his mother and father to let him go.

SEA VIEW

At last, as he had been a good boy and had worked hard at his lessons, they agreed, but said that he must promise to work at his books in his spare time. Captain McFee was pleased. He would take Tim as second ship's boy.

The first person Tim met on board was a tall, red-haired boy called Ginger. When Tim told Ginger that he was the new second ship's boy, Ginger said meanly, "Well, I am first ship's boy, so you will have to do what I tell you." However, as Tim did not seem afraid, Ginger became quite nice.

Once at sea, Tim was kept busy doing odd jobs. But when the weather was good and he had no work to do, he would sit on deck in some sunny spot and study hard. Soon he had the reputation of being a scholar.

He gave lessons in—READING AND WRITING to Ginger, who had had little schooling. ARITHMETIC to Fireman Jones, who wanted to become an engineer. HISTORY to Alaska Pete, who had a passion for King Charles I and wanted to know all about him. In the evening Tim wrote letters for Old Joe, the cook, who could not read or write at all.

Ginger I am sorry to say, was a lazy and mischievous boy. Instead of working he would hide in some corner and look at comics. When he was hungry he would steal the seamen's marmalade, and when he wished to amuse himself he teased the ship's cat which made Tim very cross because he liked cats. Now Ginger's worst mischief was to have the most terrible results for him.

The third mate was very bald. In his cabin he had many bottles filled with different-coloured hair growers. One day Ginger went to the third mate's cabin. Finding that he was out, Ginger could not resist trying all the bottles. The last bottle that Ginger tried had a very odd shape and was full of a strange-smelling green liquid. When he put it on his head, it gave him a lovely tingly feeling. Poor Ginger! Little did he know what was happening. His hair was growing and growing and GROWING.

"Bosun," roared Captain McFee when he saw Ginger, "get that boy's hair cut!"

In one hour
it was like this.

In two hours it
was like this.

From now on, everybody who saw Ginger shouted, "Go and get your hair cut!" until the boy was almost in tears.

Alaska Pete and Joe the cook spent so much time making mixtures to stop Ginger's hair from growing (the mixtures never did) that they neglected the cooking, which made the crew very cross. In fact, the ship was going to the dogs.

Ginger became so unhappy that he took to hiding in the boats. His only friends were Tim and the ship's cat.

And so things went from bad to worse.

One day the sky became cloudy and the seas began to rise. The crew grumbled about the food. The bosun was worried, and the new mixture that Pete and Joe were making smelled horrible. Tim heard Captain McFee say to the mate, "There's a hurricane blowing up or I'll eat my hat! Order all hands on deck to batten down hatches, and see that the ship's boys keep below!"

Soon the wind was blowing great guns and the waves were getting bigger and bigger, sometimes dashing over the side and wetting the crew with spray. But Ginger would not leave his hiding place.

In the meantime, Tim was sitting in the galley with Old Joe. He was terribly worried, thinking how cold and hungry Ginger must be up there in the great gale.

Finally, orders or no orders, he decided to try once more to persuade Ginger to come down.

Tim crept up the stairs and with great difficulty pushed open the door onto the deck. What he saw there made him very frightened. The sky was black with flying clouds, and great waves towered up on every side as if at any moment they would swamp the ship.

Tim dashed across the deck and just managed to reach the boat. Inside the boat was Ginger. He was cold, wet, and frightened and was holding the ship's cat in his arms.

"Come below with me," shouted Tim.

"No!" Ginger cried. "I can't, I'm too frightened!" Nothing that Tim could do or say would make him move, so Tim started back to ask the crew to help.

He had only gone a short way when a tremendous wave rushed down upon him. He leaped for the rigging and then looked around. There was no boat, no Ginger, and no cat.

Tim was horrified. "Poor Ginger, poor cat," he thought. Then in the backwash of the wave he saw the half-drowned cat floating in the water. Quickly he pulled it out and put it in the rigging.

Next he saw a great red mop of hair floating by. It was Ginger's. He grabbed it and hung on. He thought his arm would break, so hard did the rushing water try to tug Ginger away.

Captain McFee had seen them. "All hands to the rescue!" he shouted.

Alaska Pete and Old Joe tied themselves to ropes and with tremendous courage dashed across the deck and soon carried all three of them to safety.

The captain seemed furious. "How dare you disobey my orders and go on deck?" he said to Tim and Ginger. "Go below at once! Bosun," he roared, "get that boy's HAIR CUT!"

However, as they left to go, Tim saw the captain brush a tear from his eye and heard him say, "Bless those boys, Mr. Mate. Wouldn't lose them for the world. Fine boy, Tim. Fine boy."

Once the boys were below, Seaman Bloggs cut Ginger's hair. Then Pete and Joe wrapped Tim and Ginger in blankets and put them to bed. Soon they were fast asleep.

Tim woke up feeling very well. He looked at Ginger and had a great surprise. Ginger's hair had not grown at all.

"Crikey, Ginger! Look at yourself in the mirror," Tim said. You can just imagine how pleased and surprised Ginger was to see his nice short hair. Now from this time on, Ginger's hair grew in the ordinary slow way.

In a few days the sun came out, the sea was calm, and the weather became warm and fine. Tim and Ginger were back at their usual jobs and the crew were busy hanging out their clothes to dry when the captain ordered all hands to the forward well deck. There he made a speech.

"Men," he said, "during the storm the two ship's boys disobeyed my orders and nearly drowned. However, now that I have heard the full story I realise that ship's boy Tim only went on deck to rescue his friend Ginger. It was a very brave action, and I am going to ask the Royal Humane Society to give him a gold medal." (Cheers from the crew.) "Alaska Pete and Old Joe," the captain went on, "were very brave to face the raging sea and rescue the two boys and the cat. I will give them each £5." (Loud cheers.) "But I hope that in the future they will both give up making nasty-smelling mixtures and get on with the cooking." (Very loud and long cheers.)

As you can imagine, after this Tim was very popular with everyone. Ginger began to work hard, and he became quite popular, too.

From now on, the bosun took a special interest in Tim and spent much time teaching him many things that a sailor should know. Tim repeated the lessons to Ginger, who became quite clever.

But with all this you must not think that Tim neglected his lessons, because he did not.

After a long and happy voyage, the ship went back to port. Tim's mother and father were on the dock to meet him. They invited Ginger to stay with them, which he was very pleased to do as he had no home of his own.

Tim went back to school and Ginger went with him. Tim was first in Reading, Writing, Arithmetic, History, and Geography, which just goes to show how hard he had worked at his books. Ginger was second in Geography, which shows that he had worked hard, too.

But Tim's proudest moment came when there arrived by post a beautiful gold medal and a roll of fine paper on which was written the story of his brave adventure. Tim's father had the roll framed and hung it in the drawing room.

◆ LIBRARY LINK ◆

If you liked this story by Edward Ardizzone, you might enjoy reading some of his other books, such as Little Tim and the Brave Sea Captain *and* Tim and Charlotte.

Reader's Response

Imagine that you could step into this story. Where would you enter? What would you do? When would you leave?

Tim
to the Rescue

Thinking It Over

1. How did Ginger cause trouble for himself?
2. Why did Ginger hide in the boats?
3. What kind of boy was Tim?
4. Why did Tim disobey the captain?
5. What might have happened to Ginger if Tim had not gone on deck?
6. How did Ginger change after he had his frightening experience? What clues told you this?

Writing to Learn

THINK AND DECIDE Measure how you felt about each of the four parts of the story. Copy the chart and fill it in. The first part has been marked for you. Change it if you like.

Score	Tim goes to sea.	Ginger's hair grows wildly.	Tim saves Ginger.	Tim gets a medal.
very exciting				
a little exciting	X			
not exciting				

WRITE Use the chart to help you choose the most exciting part of the story. Write some sentences to tell what happened in the part you chose.

115

Until I Saw the Sea

Until I saw the sea
I did not know
that wind
could wrinkle water so.

I never knew
that sun
could splinter a whole sea of blue.

Nor
did I know before,
a sea breathes in and out
upon a shore.

Lilian Moore

117

LITERATURE LINK

How can you understand what you read?

In "Tim to the Rescue," Ginger's hair grew very fast. In two hours it grew to his waist.

Were you confused when that happened? You probably knew it was make-believe, but went along with the author—at least for the time being.

Mixing Real and Make-Believe

When a story is *all* real or *all* make-believe, it's easy to understand. But sometimes in a story that seems real, suddenly something strange happens. You're confused.

What can you do? Stop and ask yourself if the author is mixing up real and make-believe events. By doing this, the author may hope to make you laugh, give you a happy surprise, or make you notice something special. So, try believing the make-believe while you're reading. You'll understand and enjoy the story more.

How about looking at an example? Do you remember how Tim rescued Ginger? Notice how the author mixes up real and make-believe things.

> Next he saw a great red mop of hair floating by. It was Ginger's. He grabbed it and hung on. He thought his arm would break, so hard did the rushing water try to tug Ginger away.

Could a small boy really rescue someone from the huge waves by the hair? You know he couldn't. But Tim's unbelievable act makes him a bigger hero and makes the story more fun.

As you read "The Sea of Gold," you may be confused by a strange event. If you are, don't be alarmed. Just try using the following tips:

- Stop and ask yourself: Is the author mixing up real and make-believe?
- Believe the make-believe while you read, and enjoy the story!

In this folk tale, everyone laughs at Hikoichi for being kind to the fish in the sea.

The Sea of Gold

adapted by Yoshiko Uchida

On a small island, where almost everyone was a fisherman, there once lived a young man named Hikoichi (hē kō′ ē chē). He was gentle and kind, but he was slow, and there was no one on the whole island who was willing to teach him how to become a fisherman.

"How could we ever make a fisherman out of you?" people would say to him. "You are much too slow to learn anything!"

But Hikoichi wanted very badly to go to work, and he tried hard to find a job. He looked and looked for many months until finally he found work as a cook on one of the fishing boats. He got the job, however, only because no one else wanted it, but Hikoichi didn't mind. He was happy to have any kind of job at last.

Hikoichi was very careful with the food he cooked, and he tried not to waste even a single grain of rice. In fact, he hated to throw away any of the leftovers, and he stored them carefully in the galley. On the small, crowded fishing boat, however, there was no room for keeping useless things. Every bit of extra space was needed to store the catch, for the more fish they took back to the island, the more money they would all make. When the men discovered that Hikoichi was saving the leftovers, they spoke to him harshly.

"Don't use our galley space for storing garbage!" they shouted. "Throw it into the sea!"

"What a terrible waste of good food," Hikoichi thought, but he had to do as he was told. He gathered up all the leftovers he had stored and took them up on deck.

"If I must throw this into the sea," he said to himself, "I will make sure the fish have a good feast. After all, if it were not for the fish, we wouldn't be able to make a living." And so, as he threw the leftovers into the water, he called out, "Here, fish, here, good fish, have yourselves a splendid dinner!"

From that day, Hikoichi always called to the fish before he threw his leftovers into the sea. "Come along," he would call. "Enjoy some rice from my galley!" And he continued talking to them until they had eaten every morsel he tossed overboard.

The fishermen laughed when they heard him. They said, "Maybe someday the fish will answer you and tell you how much they enjoyed your dinner."

But Hikoichi didn't pay any attention to the fishermen. He silently gathered all the scraps from the table and continued to toss them out to the fish at the end of the day. Each time he did, he called to the fish as though they were his best friends, and his gentle voice echoed far out over the dancing waves of the sea.

Many years went by until Hikoichi was no longer a young man. He continued to cook for the men on his fishing boat, however, and he still fed and talked to the fish every evening.

One day, the fishing boat put far out to sea to find bigger fish. It sailed for three days and three nights, going farther and farther away from the small island. On the third night, they were still far out at sea when they dropped anchor. It was a quiet star-filled night with a full moon glowing high in the sky. The men were tired from the day's work and not long after dinner, they were all sound asleep.

Hikoichi, however, still had much to do. He scrubbed the pots, cleaned up the galley and washed the rice for breakfast. When he had finished, he gathered all the leftovers in a basket and went up on deck.

"Gather around, good fish," he called as always. "Enjoy your dinner."

He emptied his basket and stayed to watch the fish eat up his food. Then, he went to his bunk to prepare for bed, but somehow the boat felt very strange. It had stopped rolling. In fact, it was not moving at all and felt as though it were standing on dry land.

"That's odd," Hikoichi thought, and he ran up on deck to see what had happened. He leaned over the railing and looked out.

"What!" he shouted. "The ocean is gone!"

And indeed it had disappeared. There was not a single drop of water anywhere. As far as Hikoichi could see, there was nothing but miles and miles of sand. It was as though the boat were standing in the middle of a huge desert of shimmering sand.

Hikoichi could not believe his eyes. He simply had to get off the boat to see if they really were standing on dry land. Slowly, he lowered himself down a rope ladder and reached the sand below. Carefully, he took a step and felt his foot crunch on something. No, it wasn't water. It really was sand after all. Hikoichi blinked as he looked around, for under the light of the moon, the sand glittered and sparkled like a beach of gold. He scooped up a handful and watched it glisten as it slid through his fingers.

"Why, this is beautiful," Hikoichi thought, and his heart sang with joy at the sight. "I must save some of this sand so I can remember this wonderful night forever." He hurried back onto the boat for a bucket, filled it with sparkling sand and then carried it aboard and hid it carefully beneath his bunk. He looked around at the other men, but they were all sound asleep. Not one seemed to have noticed that the boat was standing still. Hikoichi slipped quietly into his bunk, and soon he too was sound asleep.

The next morning Hikoichi was the first to wake up. He remembered the amazing happening of the night before, and he leaped out of bed, ready to call the other men to see the strange sight. But as he got dressed, he felt the familiar rocking of the boat. He hurried up on deck and he saw that once again they were out in the middle of the ocean with waves all about them. Hikoichi shook his head, but now he could no longer keep it all to himself. As soon as the other men came up on deck, he told his story.

"It's true," he cried as he saw wide grins appear on the men's faces. "The ocean was gone and for miles and miles there was nothing but sand. It glittered and sparkled under the full moon and it was as though we were sailing on a sea of golden sand!"

The men roared with laughter. "Hikoichi, you were surely dreaming," they said. "Now put away your daydreams and fix us some breakfast."

"No, no, I wasn't dreaming," Hikoichi cried. "I climbed down the ladder and I walked on the sand. I picked it up and felt it slip through my fingers. It wasn't a dream. It really wasn't."

It was then that Hikoichi remembered his bucket. "Wait! Come with me and I can prove it," he said, and he led the men down to his bunk. Then, getting down on his hands and knees, he carefully pulled out his bucket of sand. "There," he said proudly, "I scooped this up when I went down and walked on the sand. Now do you believe me?"

The men suddenly stopped laughing. "This isn't sand," they said, reaching out to feel it. "It's gold! It's a bucket full of pure gold!"

"Why didn't you get more?" one of the men shouted.

"You've got to give some of it to us," another added.

"We share our fish with you. You must share your gold with us," said still another.

Soon all the men were yelling and shouting and pushing to get their hands on Hikoichi's bucket of gold.

Then the oldest of the fishermen spoke up. "Stop it! Stop it!" he called out. "This gold doesn't belong to any of you. It belongs to Hikoichi."

He reminded the men how Hikoichi had fed the fish of the sea for so many years as though they were his own children.

"Now the King of the Sea has given Hikoichi a reward for his kindness to the fish," he explained. And turning to Hikoichi, he added, "You are gentle and kind and good. This gift from the Kingdom of the Sea is your reward. Take all the gold and keep it, for it belongs only to you."

The shouting, pushing fishermen suddenly became silent and thoughtful, for they knew the old fisherman was right. They were ashamed of having laughed at Hikoichi year after year, and they knew that he truly deserved this fine reward.

Without another word the men went back to work. They completed their catch that day and the heavily laden boat returned once more to the little island.

The next time the boat put out to sea, Hikoichi was no longer aboard, for now he had enough gold to leave his job forever. He built himself a beautiful new house, and he even had a small boat of his own so he could still sail out to sea and feed the fish. He used his treasure from the sea wisely and well, and he lived a long and happy life.

◆ LIBRARY LINK ◆

If you enjoyed this story by Yoshiko Uchida, you might enjoy reading other books written by the author. A few titles are The Best Bad Thing *and* Sumi's Special Happening.

Reader's Response

What did you think of Hikoichi? Would you like him to be your friend? Why?

The Sea of Gold

Thinking It Over

1. Why did Hikoichi feed the fish?
2. What unusual event took place one night?
3. What made Hikoichi so happy on that special night?
4. Why do you think the King of the Sea waited until late at night to do his magic? How did you get your answer?
5. How did the reward affect Hikoichi's life? What was the same? What was different?

Writing to Learn

THINK AND CONNECT In Hikoichi's story, one thing leads to another. Read the first ''thought link'' below. Then copy and finish the second ''thought link.''

Because he fed the fish, — he found sand of pure gold.

Because he had gold, —

WRITE Make up your own ''thought link'' about a happy day you remember? In the first link write ''Because ___,'' and in the second link write ''I had a happy day.'' Finish the first link with your own words.

131

Who can dive into the deepest ocean and see in the watery darkness? You and I can't, but Alvin and Jason Jr. can!

The Wonderful Underwater Machine

by Josephine Edgar

A team of engineers and scientists at the Woods Hole Oceanographic Institution in Massachusetts wanted to study the deepest parts of the ocean. They knew it was impossible for people to survive outside a submarine in the deepest parts of the ocean, so the team worked together to build a machine called Jason Jr., or "JJ" for short.

If you saw Jason Jr., swimming at the bottom of the ocean, you might think you were looking at a big, blue bug with two bright eyes. But JJ is not a bug, and its bright eyes are really two bright lights! JJ is a small machine, only twenty-eight inches long, but it is capable of swimming deep in the ocean.

Deep under the ocean, the weight of the water pushes down very hard on anything found on the ocean floor. Sometimes there are sharp rocks and coral that can harm and even tear apart a machine. So the engineers knew they had to make JJ strong. The engineers could not make all of JJ's parts out of metal though, because a heavy metal machine would sink to the bottom of the ocean. They solved this problem by making a special skin for JJ.

The outside of JJ's skin is made of blue fiberglass. The fiberglass covers millions of tiny glass balls. These balls are smaller than grains of sand, and each ball has air inside, like a tiny bubble. The balls are glued together and help JJ float in the water. The tiny glass balls are also hard like marbles. When JJ bumps into something sharp, the balls protect it.

This is Jason Jr., also referred to as JJ. If you saw JJ in the water, what would you think it was?

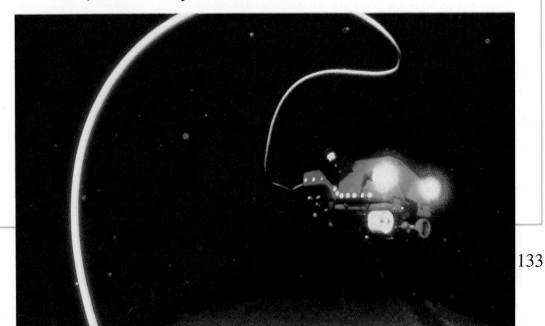

133

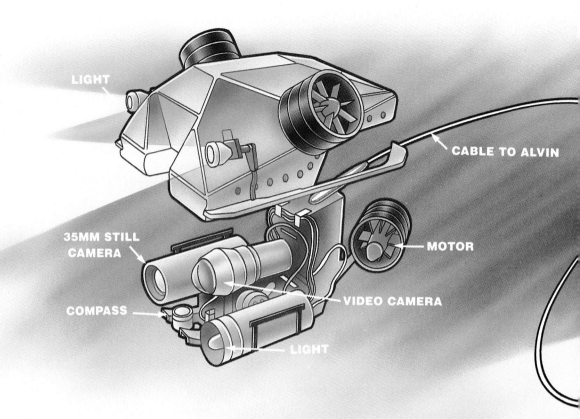

LIGHT

CABLE TO ALVIN

35MM STILL CAMERA

MOTOR

COMPASS

VIDEO CAMERA

LIGHT

JJ's protective cover has been lifted so you can see how it looks inside.

Inside JJ are motors that help it move and two cameras that take pictures of what it sees.

Behind JJ is a long cable that looks like a tail. This cable is more than 200 feet long. Because it's bendable, JJ can swim in any direction. The cable is also very strong, and it keeps the wires inside it safe and dry. These wires are very important, because the scientists use them to send signals to JJ that tell the machine what to do. The wires also send television pictures and signals back to the scientists. The signals tell what JJ finds.

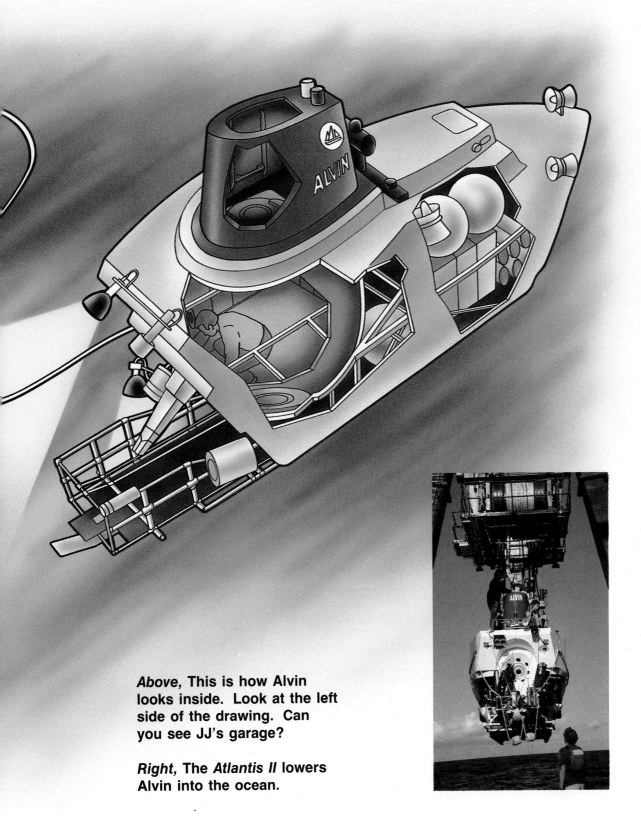

Above, This is how Alvin looks inside. Look at the left side of the drawing. Can you see JJ's garage?

Right, The *Atlantis II* lowers Alvin into the ocean.

135

Atlantis II **stands by while Alvin takes JJ down to the ocean bottom to explore and to take pictures.**

To get to the bottom of the ocean, Jason Jr., gets a ride from Alvin. Alvin is a submarine that can dive in very deep water. It carries JJ in a small garage, which is just under the front window. Inside Alvin there is room for two scientists and a pilot who drives the submarine.

The scientists use a big ship named *Atlantis II* to take Alvin and JJ out into the ocean. Then, *Atlantis II* lowers Alvin into the water, and the submarine starts to go down.

Alvin drops quickly because the scientists have put heavy steel weights on Alvin to make it sink. In one minute, Alvin can fall 100 feet. As Alvin goes down, the water gets darker and darker. First the ocean is blue. Then it is dark blue. In fifteen minutes, it is so dark that the scientists must turn on the lights inside Alvin to see. It is dark because sunlight can't reach the deepest parts of the ocean.

The scientists can't see the bottom, but they can tell when they are getting close to it by using Alvin's sonar. The sonar machine makes a noise and listens for the noise to bounce off the ocean floor. When the scientists hear the echo a short time after the noise is made, they know that the ocean floor is close.

Alvin's sonar tells scientists how close it is to the ocean bottom. This diagram shows how sonar works.

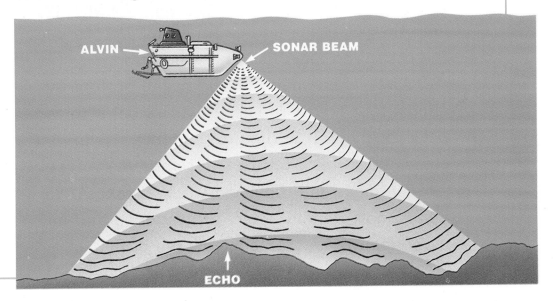

ALVIN →   SONAR BEAM

ECHO

When they are near to the bottom, the scientists drop one of Alvin's heavy weights. This makes Alvin slow down. Then, as they let go of more weights, Alvin settles down softly in the mud at the bottom. Using Alvin's lights, the scientists can see out of the small windows. Now, they are ready to use Jason Jr., to get a closer look.

Next, JJ swims out pulling its cable behind it. The scientists signal JJ where to look. It shines its lights on whatever the scientists are studying and takes pictures. JJ sends the pictures back to the scientists through the cable, which is also attached to Alvin.

The scientists are using JJ to look closely at rocks and mountains in the deepest parts of the ocean. They are learning where we can find important metals. They are also using JJ to study fish and other living things. JJ's pictures help the scientists understand how we can use the oceans to raise fish and other food.

After JJ has been on the ocean bottom for almost four hours, the scientists signal it to come back to Alvin. It is time to go home. Alvin comes back up to return to *Atlantis II.*

The next day the scientists will take Alvin and JJ down again. They are eager to find out more about what lies beneath the ocean.

In 1986 the scientists from the Woods Hole Oceanographic Institution used JJ to explore a famous ship that sank to the bottom of the ocean many years ago. In 1912 this large ship hit an iceberg and sank. The ship was the *Titanic*.

The scientists wanted to test JJ to find out how well it could swim inside the ship and take pictures. JJ did very well. It even swam down stairs and looked into rooms. The scientists sitting inside Alvin could see the pictures that JJ sent back. The pictures showed ceiling lamps and an old, rusty bathtub, but all the wooden furniture and stairs were gone. The scientists guessed that small shellfish had eaten anything wooden. The pictures also showed cups and bottles resting on the ocean bottom next to the shipwreck.

JJ approaches the sunken *Titanic*. Scientists were able to see the inside of the ship from the pictures JJ took.

JJ took this photograph of the *Titanic's* deck. How can you tell the ship has been underwater for a long time?

Engineers at Woods Hole are now building newer and bigger machines like Jason Jr., and Alvin. Some of these machines will help them make better maps of the mountains and valleys on the ocean floor. Others will give us closer looks at shipwrecks. The underwater machines of the future will help scientists learn more about our oceans so that we can use them safely and wisely.

Reader's Response

What is it about undersea exploration that sounds exciting to you?

The Wonderful Underwater Machine

Thinking It Over

1. What problems did the engineers have to think about when they made Jason Jr.?
2. How does Alvin's sonar machine help scientists?
3. What would happen if JJ's cable were to break? How do you know?
4. Why is it important for scientists to learn about the ocean?
5. In what ways do you think scientists might use JJ to study the bottom of the ocean in the future?

Writing to Learn

THINK AND IMAGINE   Imagine you are in the submarine Alvin, using JJ to take pictures. Draw JJ, its long cable, and a sea creature it may be photographing.

WRITE   Write sentences to describe your creature of the deep. What color is it? What shape? How big? Is its skin scaly or slippery?

LITERATURE LINK

How do headings help you read?

In "The Wonderful Underwater Machine," the author uses diagrams and pictures to show how Jason Jr. works. They help you learn new information.

Look quickly at the article below. Even before you read it, you can learn about whales from the picture. What else can help you learn about whales?

Whales Are Mammals

Breathing Air

Whales are mammals, so they must breathe air. They can dive under the water, but they must always return to the surface for air. A whale's nose is called a "blowhole." It is on top of the whale's head, so the whale can breathe without coming very far out of the water.

Staying Warm

Whales often swim in very cold water. To help them stay warm, they have a thick layer of fat around their bodies. This is called "blubber." It acts like an overcoat to keep heat inside the body from escaping.

—John Bonnett Wexo, *Whales*

Headings Help

The article has phrases called headings at the beginning of each paragraph. Headings break the information into smaller parts. What can you learn just by reading the headings?

The headings in this article help you know that whales must breathe air and stay warm. And that is exactly what you will learn from reading this article. You've already learned a lot and you haven't read the whole article yet!

When you read an article with headings, try using these tips. They will help you organize your reading and learn new information.

- Read all the headings.
- Think about what you learn from them.
- Read the section under each heading.
- Stop after each section to sum up important details.

Try the tips for using headings as you read "Seals on the Land and in the Water." See if they help you learn and remember the information in the article.

Some animals live on land. Some live in the water. The amazing seal is at home in both places!

SEALS

On the Land and in the Water

by Betsey Knafo

What do a seal and an elephant have in common? They are both mammals. Other mammals include cats, dogs, horses, people, whales, and dolphins. All mammals are alike in certain ways. They are warm-blooded and breathe air with their lungs. Their bodies are covered with hair or fur. Their babies are born, not hatched from eggs like birds and reptiles. Baby mammals also drink milk from their mothers.

Most mammals, like people, live on land. Some mammals, like whales and dolphins, live only in the water. Still other mammals, like seals, live both on land and in the water.

Seals in the Water

The bodies of seals are filled with strong muscles. These strong muscles and the seals' flippers help them move through water swiftly and easily.

◀ This harbor seal enjoys the sun.
A fur seal takes time to rest. ▶

145

Seals are shaped like long footballs. Blubber, or fat, under their skin gives them this odd shape. Blubber is important to help the seals survive. Most seals live in the icy, cold waters around the North and South Poles. Unlike fish who swim in the same cold waters, seals are warm-blooded. They need the blubber to keep them warm as they swim in the cold water or walk on the ice. Blubber also gives them extra energy.

Most seals can stay underwater for at least twenty minutes, and some can even stay under for almost an hour! Then they need to come up for air. How does a seal hold its breath so long? A seal's heartbeat slows down underwater, so it needs less air underwater than it does on land.

When swimming under ice, seals make breathing holes in the ice. They make these holes by chewing with their teeth and scratching with their claws or by using their warm breath to melt the ice.

Seals can even sleep underwater. If the water is not too deep, they sink to the bottom and rise to the top to get air when they need it. In deep water they sleep with just their noses above the water.

An elephant seal swims off the coast of California.

This mother harbor seal stays close to her pup.

Seals get their food from the water by diving deep under the water for fish and shellfish. Some seals have been known to dive so deep that they have brought up fish that most people have never seen before.

Seals on the Land 〜〜〜

Seals have no feet or legs, so they must use their flippers to move around on land. They can move quickly on land, but they are faster and more graceful in water. The same flippers that help them glide through the water appear clumsy and awkward on rocks and ice.

One reason seals come out of the water is to rest. Depending on where they live, they can be found on rocks, sand, or ice. They choose spots to rest where they can easily get back into the water.

Another reason seals live on land is to have babies. These babies are called pups. Usually only one pup is born at a time.

147

Nature helps protect the pups. The colors of their fur match the colors of their surroundings. In cold climates, the pups have white fur to match the ice around them. In warmer climates, the pups have dark fur to match the land and rocks. Most pups cannot swim for at least one month, so they must stay on land. The color of their coats helps protect baby seals from their enemies, because if the enemies cannot see the pups, they cannot harm them.

This is a baby harp seal.

Living in Two Worlds 〜〜〜

Water is where seals move with greatest ease, and water is where seals find their food. However, seals cannot survive by living in water alone. Seals need to be on land for resting and giving birth to baby seals. Seals are mammals that must survive in the two worlds of land and water.

◆ LIBRARY LINK ◆

If you would like to read about other sea animals, try Sea Otters *by Evelyn Shaw and* Little Whale *by Ann McGovern.*

Reader's Response

What piece of information about seals did you find most interesting?

Seals
On the Land and in the Water

Thinking It Over

1. Where are most seals found?
2. Which parts of a seal's body help it survive icy land and water?
3. Why do seals stay close to the water when they are on land? How did you find the answer?
4. The author says that seals are clumsy on land. Do you agree? Describe how they look.
5. What is the main idea in this article about seals?

Writing to Learn

THINK AND RECALL   Seals in the water behave differently from seals on land. Make a chart to show three differences. Copy and finish the chart below.

Seals

	In the Water	On the Land
How They Move	They move gracefully.	
How They Breathe		They breathe normally.
How They Sleep		They sleep well.

WRITE   Write one paragraph about seals on land. Write another about seals in the water. Use the information in your chart to help you.

149

The Monkey and the CROCODILE

A Jataka Tale from India

written and illustrated by Paul Galdone

Watch out, monkey! Here comes crocodile!

Beside a river in the jungle stood a tall mango tree. In the tree lived many monkeys. They swung from branch to branch, eating fruit and chattering to each other.

Hungry crocodiles swam in the river and sunned themselves on the banks.

One young crocodile was hungrier than all the rest. He could never get enough to eat.

The young crocodile watched the monkeys for a long time. Then one day he said to a wise old crocodile: "I'd like to catch a monkey and eat him!"

"How would you ever catch a monkey?" asked the old crocodile. "You do not travel on land and monkeys do not go into the water. Besides, they are quicker than you are."

"They may be quicker," said the young crocodile, "but I am more cunning. You will see!"

For days the crocodile swam back and forth, studying the monkeys all the while.

151

Then he noticed one young monkey who was quicker than all the others. This monkey loved to jump to the highest branches of the tree and pick the ripe mangos at the very top.

"He's the one I want," the crocodile said to himself. "But how am I going to catch him?"

The crocodile thought and thought, and at last he had an idea.

"Monkey," he called, "wouldn't you like to come with me over to the island, where the fruit is so ripe?"

"Oh, yes," said the monkey. "But how can I go with you? I do not swim."

"I will take you on my back," said the crocodile, with a toothy smile.

The monkey was eager to get to the fruit, so he jumped down on the crocodile's back.

"Off we go!" said the crocodile, gliding through the water.

"This is a fine ride you are giving me," said the monkey.

"Do you think so? Well, how do you like this?" asked the crocodile. And suddenly he dived down into the water.

"Oh, please don't!" cried the monkey as he went under. He was afraid to let go and he did not know what to do.

When the crocodile came up, the monkey sputtered and choked. "Why did you take me under water, Crocodile?" he asked. "You know I can't swim!"

"Because I am going to drown you," replied the crocodile. "And then I am going to eat you."

The monkey shivered in fear. But he thought quickly and before the crocodile dived again, he said: "I wish you had told me you wanted to eat me. If I had known that, I would have brought my heart."

"Your heart?" asked the crocodile.

"Yes, it is the tastiest part of me. But I left it behind in the tree."

"Then we must go back and get it," said the crocodile, turning around.

"But we are so near the island," said the monkey. "Please take me there first."

"No," said the crocodile. "First I am taking you straight to your tree. You will get your heart and bring it to me at once. Then we will see about going to the island."

"Very well," said the monkey.

And the crocodile headed back to the river bank.

No sooner did the monkey jump onto the bank than up he swung into the tree. From the highest branch he called down to the crocodile: "My heart is way up here. If you want it, come for it! Come for it!" And he laughed and laughed while the crocodile thrashed his tail in anger.

That night the monkey moved far down river from the mango tree. He wanted to get away from the crocodile so he could live in peace.

But the crocodile was still determined to catch him. He searched and searched and finally he found the monkey, living in another tree.

Here a large rock rose out of the water, halfway between the monkey's new home and the island. The crocodile watched the monkey jumping from the river bank to the rock, and then to the island where the fruit trees were.

"Monkey will stay on the island all day," the crocodile thought to himself. "And I'll catch him on his way home tonight."

The monkey had a fine feast, while the crocodile swam about, watching him all day. Toward night, the crocodile crawled out of the water and lay on the rock, perfectly still.

When it grew dark among the trees, the monkey started for home. He ran down to the river bank, and there he stopped.

"What is the matter with the rock?" the monkey wondered. "I never saw it so high before. Something must be lying on it."

The monkey went to the water's edge and called: "Hello, Rock!"

No answer.

He called again: "Hello, Rock!"

Still no answer.

Three times the monkey called, and then he said: "Why is it, friend Rock, that you do not answer me tonight?"

"Oh," said the crocodile to himself, "the rock must talk to the monkey at night. I'll have to answer for the rock this time."

So he answered: "Yes, Monkey! What is it?"

The monkey laughed and said: "Oh, it's you, Crocodile, is it?"

"Yes," said the crocodile. "I am waiting here for you. And I am going to eat you up!"

"You have certainly caught me this time," said the monkey, sounding afraid. "There is no other way for me to go home. Open your mouth wide so I can jump right into it."

Now the monkey knew very well that when crocodiles open their mouths wide, they shut their eyes.

So while the crocodile lay on the rock with his mouth open and his eyes shut, the monkey jumped.

But not into his mouth!

He landed on the top of the crocodile's head, and then sprang quickly to the river bank.

Up he ran into his tree.

When the crocodile saw the trick the monkey had played on him, he said: "Monkey, I thought I was cunning, but you are much more cunning than I. And you know no fear. I will leave you alone after this."

"Thank you, Crocodile," said the monkey. "But I shall be on the watch for you just the same."

And so he was, and the crocodile never, never caught him.

Reader's Response

If you could be either the monkey or the crocodile, which would you choose? Why?

The Monkey and the CROCODILE

 ## Thinking It Over

1. Why was it so hard for a crocodile to catch a monkey?
2. How did the crocodile get the monkey to come to him?
3. Why did the crocodile think the monkey wouldn't see him on the rock?
4. List some of the ways the monkey proved he was clever. What clues did you use to make your list?
5. Do you think that the monkey should trust the crocodile to leave him alone?

 ## Writing to Learn

THINK AND IMAGINE   Do you think the crocodile will ever stop trying to catch the monkey? Do you think the monkey could catch the crocodile? Look at the picture below and imagine what might happen next time they meet.

WRITE   Write a new ending for this story. Tell how the monkey catches the crocodile.

How Doth the

Little Crocodile

How doth the little crocodile
    Improve his shining tail,
And pour the waters of the Nile
    On every golden scale!

How cheerfully he seems to grin,
    How neatly spreads his claws,
And welcomes little fishes in,
    With gently smiling jaws!

Lewis Carroll

WORLD OF READING

Magazine

News About Reading

Sea Shanties

Long ago, sailors sang songs as they worked on ships. Often they had to work for long hours, pulling heavy ropes. Singing helped them pull the ropes in time together.

A sailor's work song was called a *shanty*. (Sometimes the word is spelled *chanty* or *chantey*.) Each ship had a Shanty Man, or best singer, who helped keep the sailors together. The Shanty Man had a good sense of humor and an ability to make up verses to songs.

Sailors working on a ship in the 1890s

The Shanty Man would sing a verse. Then the sailors would chant, or sing back, in a lively chorus.

Here are some of the words to a famous, old sea shanty called "Blow the Man Down."

SHANTY MAN: *Blow the man down, bullies, blow the man down!*

SAILORS: *To me way-aye blow the man down.*

SHANTY MAN: *Oh blow the man down, bullies, blow the man down.*

SAILORS: *Give me some time to blow the man down!*

"Blow the Man Down" has many verses that were sung over and over to help build cooperation and spirit during long voyages. Verses were added and changed over the years, but the familiar melody remains the same today.

If you are interested in learning the verses to this song, or other sea shanties, such as "Shenandoah" or "Rio Grande," look in the library for a songbook called *Fireside Book of Folk Songs*.

> ☛ *What if you want to learn the tune to a song but you cannot read musical notes? Ask your librarian to help you find songs on records or tapes.*

Funny sounds come from the house on East 88th Street. . . . and that's strange because no one lives there!

The House on East 88th Street

written and illustrated by Bernard Waber

This is the house. The house on East 88th Street. It is empty now, but it won't be for long. Strange sounds come from the house. Can you hear them? Listen: SWISH, SWASH, SPLASH, SWOOSH . . .

It began one sunny morning when the Citywide Storage and Moving Company truck pulled up to the house on East 88th Street and unloaded the belongings of Mr. and Mrs. Joseph F. Primm and their young son Joshua. It was a trying day for everyone. Mrs. Primm just couldn't decide where to put the piano. And Mr. Primm's favorite hat was accidentally packed away in one of dozens of cartons lying about.

SWISH, SWASH, SPLASH, SWOOSH. Loudly
and clearly the sounds now rumbled through the
house. "It's only a little thunder," Mrs. Primm
assured everyone. When a Citywide Storage and
Moving man carried in their potted pistachio
tree, everyone rejoiced; the truck was at last
empty. The movers wished them well and
hurried off to their next job for the day.

"Now, I'm going to prepare our lunch," announced Mrs. Primm. "But first I want to go upstairs and wash these grimy hands."

SWISH, SWASH, SPLASH, SWOOSH . . .

A puzzled Mrs. Primm stopped to listen. By and by her ears directed her to the bathroom door.

"What can it be?" she asked herself as she opened the door.

What she saw made her slam it quickly shut.

Mrs. Primm knew she was going to scream and just waited for it to happen. But she couldn't scream. She could scarcely even talk. The most Mrs. Primm was able to manage was the sharp hoarse whisper of a voice which she used to call Mr. Primm.

"Joseph," she said, "there's a crocodile in our bathtub."

Mr. Primm looked into the bathroom.

The next moment found them flying off in different directions.

"Help, help," Mrs. Primm cried out as she struggled with a window stuck with fresh paint.

"Operator, operator," Mr. Primm shouted into the telephone, and then he remembered that it was not yet connected.

Joshua, who had heard everything, raced to the front door, to be greeted there by an oddly dressed man who handed him a note. "This will explain everything about the crocodile," said the man, leaving quietly but swiftly.

Mr. Primm read the note:

Please be kind to my crocodile.
He is the most gentle of creatures
and would not do harm to a flea.
He must have tender, loving care,
for he is an artist and can perform
many good tricks. Perhaps he will
perform some for you.

I shall return.

Cordially,

Hector P. Valenti
Star of stage and screen

P.S. He will eat only Turkish caviar.
P.P.S. His name is Lyle.

"Turkish caviar indeed," exclaimed Mrs. Primm. "Oh, to think this could happen on East 88th Street. Whatever will we do with him?"

Suddenly, before anyone could think of a worthy answer, there was Lyle.

And just as suddenly he got hold of a ball that had been lying among Joshua's belongings and began to balance it on his nose . . . and roll it down the notches of his spine.

Now he was walking on his front feet . . . and taking flying leaps.

Now he was twirling Joshua's hoop, doing it so expertly that the Primms just had to clap their hands and laugh.

Lyle bowed appreciatively.

He had won his way into their hearts and into their new home.

"Every home should have a crocodile," said Mrs. Primm one day.

"Lyle is one of the family now. He loves helping out with chores."

"He won't allow anyone else to carry out old newspapers . . . or take in the milk."

"He folds towels, feeds the bird, and when he sets the table there is always a surprise."

"I had only to show him once how to make up a bed."

"People everywhere stop to talk with him. They say he is the nicest crocodile they ever met."

"Lyle likes to play in the park. He always goes once around in the pony cart."

"And now he has learned to eat something besides Turkish caviar."

"Lyle is a good sport. Everyone wants him to play on his side."

"He is wonderful company. We take him everywhere."

"Just give him his Turkish caviar and his bed of warm water and he is happy as a bird."

One day a brass band paraded past the house on East 88th Street.

The Primm family rushed to the window to watch. They called for Lyle, but there was no answer.

"Look," someone pointed out. "It's Lyle, he's in the parade."

There was Lyle doing his specialty of somersault, flying leaps, walking on front feet and taking bows just as he did the first day they laid eyes on him. The people watching cheered him on, while Lyle smiled back at them and blew kisses. A photographer was on hand to take pictures.

The next day Lyle was famous.

The telephone rang continually and bundles of mail were dropped by the door. One letter was from someone Lyle knew particularly well. Mr. Primm read it:

Just a few words to say
I shall return.

Cordially,

Hector P. Valenti
Star of stage and screen

P.S. Very soon.
P.P.S. To fetch my crocodile.

Several days later, Mrs. Primm and Lyle
were in the kitchen shelling peas when they
heard a knocking at the door.

It was Hector P. Valenti, star of stage and
screen.

"I have come for Lyle," announced Signor
Valenti.

"You can't have Lyle," cried Mrs. Primm, "he
is very happy living here, and we love him
dearly."

"Lyle must be returned to me," insisted Signor Valenti. "Was it not I who raised him from young crocodilehood? Was it not I who taught him his bag of tricks? We have appeared together on stages the world over."

"But why then did you leave him alone in a strange house?" asked Mrs. Primm.

"Because," answered Signor Valenti, "I could no longer afford to pay for his Turkish caviar. But now Lyle is famous and we shall be very rich." Mrs. Primm was saddened, but she knew Lyle properly belonged to Signor Valenti and she had to let him go.

It was a tearful parting for everyone.

Signor Valenti had big plans for Lyle. They were to travel far and wide . . . stay in many hotels . . . where sometimes the tubs were too big . . . and other times too small . . . or too crowded.

Signor Valenti did what he could to coax a smile from Lyle.

He tried making funny faces at him . . . he stood on his head. He tickled his toes and told him uproarious stories that in happier days would have had Lyle doubled over with laughter.

But Lyle could not laugh. Nor could he make people laugh. He made them cry instead . . . One night in Paris, he made an entire audience cry.

The theater manager was furious and ordered them off his stage.

Meanwhile at the house on East 88th Street, Mrs. Primm went about her work without her usual bright smile. And deep sighs could be heard coming from behind the newspaper Mr. Primm was reading.

Every morning Joshua anxiously awaited the arrival of the mailman in hope of receiving word from Lyle. One morning a letter did come. He knew the handwriting very well.

Just a few words to say
we shall return.

Cordially,

Hector P. Valenti

Hector P. Valenti

Former star of stage and screen

P.S. I am sick of crocodiles.
P.P.S. And the tears of crocodiles.

Not too many days after, the Primms were delighted to find Hector P. Valenti and Lyle at their door.

"Here, take him back," said Signor Valenti. "He is no good. He will never make anyone laugh again."

But Signor Valenti was very much mistaken.

Everyone laughed . . . and laughed . . . and laughed.

And in the end so did Signor Valenti.

So now if you should happen to be walking past the house on East 88th Street and if you should happen to hear sounds that go: SWISH, SWASH, SPLASH, SWOOSH! don't be surprised. It's only Lyle. Lyle the crocodile.

◆ LIBRARY LINK ◆

If you like this story by Bernard Waber, you might enjoy reading some of his other books, such as I Was All Thumbs, The Snake, A Very Long Story, *and* An Anteater Named Arthur.

Reader's Response

How did you feel when Lyle left the Primms? Were you angry with Mr. Valenti? Tell why or why not.

Writing Dialogue

In the stories you have just read, characters talk to one another. What characters say to one another can help you understand how they feel. When you read what characters say to each other you are reading dialogue. Read this dialogue.

"How would you ever catch a monkey?" asked the old crocodile. "You do not travel on land and monkeys do not go into the water. Besides, they are quicker than you are."

"They may be quicker," said the young crocodile, "but I am more cunning. You will see!"

Think about a piece of dialogue you could write between two animals in the stories you have read.

Prewriting

Imagine a dialogue between two sharks, or other sea creatures, when they see Jason Jr., the wonderful underwater machine. Make a chart like the one on the next page, and use it to plan your dialogue.

A Dialogue Between Animals	
First Shark Says	"Do you see what I see?"
Second Shark Says	
First Shark Says	
Second Shark Says	

Writing

Make up the rest of the dialogue between the two sharks. Start a new paragraph when there is a different speaker. Add more statements to finish the dialogue.

Revising

Read your dialogue again. Does it sound like a real conversation? Add more details if they are needed. Would using a synonym for one of the words make the dialogue sound more natural?

Proofreading

Check to make sure you used quotation marks at the beginning and end of each speaker's words. Make a neat copy.

Publishing

See if others in your class wrote dialogue about the same character you chose. If so, display them together.

Making a Watery World Collage

Stories in this unit told you many things about life in or near the water. You learned how seals live. You also read about an underwater vehicle named JJ. Your group will now make a collage that shows water scenes from this unit.

As you work together, do one or more of these jobs:

◆ Give your ideas to the group.

◆ Ask others to talk.

◆ Thank people for their ideas.

◆ Help the group finish on time.

Start by talking together about the stories in this unit. As a group, choose the stories you would like to show on your "Watery World" collage. Then, take turns giving ideas about animals, people, boats, or other vehicles from the stories that might go on your collage. Each of you should choose one thing to draw for the collage. When you have finished your drawing, cut it out. Take turns pasting the cut-out drawings on a large sheet of paper. Finally, add details like fish, rocks, or waves to finish your collage.

Will your friends know which stories you picked for your "Watery World" collage?

Amy Goes Fishing by Jean Marzollo *(Dial, 1980)* Amy is not at all sure that spending a Saturday fishing with her father is going to be very exciting, but a lunch and a "catch" change her view.

A First Look at Seashells by Millicent E. Selsam and Joyce Hunt *(Walker, 1983)* This book identifies the two main groups of shells, asks questions about them, and uses black-and-white drawings to help the reader answer the questions.

Little Whale by Ann McGovern *(Scholastic, 1979)* Follow a humpback whale from its birth to being full-grown. What whales eat, where they travel, and how humans have acted toward whales are also covered in this book.

Sea Songs by Myra Cohn Livingston *(Holiday, 1986)* This book has poems about sea life.

ON YOUR OWN

1

It can be fun to do things on your own.

What makes some people so good at being on their own?

BOY JUGGLING SHELLS,
*ink and color on paper by Katsushika Hokusai,
Japanese, (1760–1849)*

183

Jason has a dream. To make his dream come true, he will have to do something that even most grown-ups couldn't do.

Jason
Wants
a Library

by
Margaret Tuley Patton

Every time ten-year-old Jason Hardman wanted a book from a library, he borrowed his sister's bike and pedaled six miles to the next town, Monroe. Since Jason's favorite thing to do was to read books, he spent hours pedaling.

Jason's town of Elsinore, Utah, had only 650 people, too tiny for a library of its own. Elsinore was so small that the children even went to school in Monroe.

One night, Jason said to his parents, "I want to start a library in Elsinore." They were pleased but told him that he would have to talk with the town council.

This is Jason, the boy who wants a library.

"What is a town council?" Jason asked.

"It's a group of about eight elected members and the mayor. They run all the town's business," his mom said. "Elsinore, like all towns, collects taxes from its citizens and uses the money for public services, such as fire and police protection," she explained.

"But the town can't afford a library," his dad added.

"Maybe I can run it for the town," Jason said.

Talking to nine adults sounded scary, but Jason wanted to give it a try.

On the night of the next council meeting, he and his father went to the town hall. A two-storied stone building constructed in the 1890s, White Rock School was now the town hall. There in a large room he found the council members sitting around an oval table talking about town matters. They barely looked up when Jason came into the room. The council was talking about the new fire engine and how to fix the roads. The mayor, a thin, serious-looking man, sometimes looked over in Jason's direction. A council member, a gray-haired woman with large gold earrings, also watched him.

When it was Jason's time, *everyone* looked at him. At first he hesitated, then began to speak. "I want to start a library in Elsinore. It needs one very badly."

The council listened closely. Jason spent almost an hour talking with the council.

"We'll have to think about it," the mayor finally said to the brown-haired boy.

"At least they didn't say no," Jason told his parents after the meeting.

A week went by without any news from the town hall. Jason phoned the mayor at his home to ask if a decision had been made about the library. The mayor answered, "The council is still thinking about it."

Another week passed. Every day when Jason came off the school bus, he'd ask his mother: "Did the mayor phone?" Each day, the answer was, "No." Jason phoned the mayor every night for two weeks. Each night, the same answer was given: "The council is still thinking about it." Jason grew tired of waiting. Why can't I use the town hall basement for my library? he thought to himself.

During those weeks, Jason pedaled often to Monroe for library books. "I wonder if I will be biking these six miles forever for a book?" he asked himself sadly. He began to doubt that he would ever get a library for Elsinore.

At last it happened. When he phoned the mayor, Jason was invited to the council's next meeting. The mayor told him they might find space in the town hall basement. It was just too good to be true.

When Jason wanted library books, he pedaled six miles.

When Jason entered the council room and saw them all sitting at the oval table, he suddenly felt terrible. He just knew that they had changed their minds. The mayor, with a stern face, turned toward Jason and asked him to come to the oval table. Jason sat down in the straight-back chair.

The council began asking him questions. Someone asked how many days the library would be open. "Tuesdays and Thursdays from 4 to 6 P.M.," Jason answered quietly.

At last, the mayor looked across the table and said in a firm voice, "After weeks of thinking, we have decided that you can use a room in the basement for a public library."

Jason was so shocked he could hardly speak. Now all the council members and the mayor smiled and wished him good luck. "We figure that you can run a library the right way, and we want to give you the chance," the mayor said. Jason almost danced out of the meeting.

In the next few weeks, Jason told every person he knew in Elsinore that he was opening a library in the town hall. He went to the Elsinore Literary Club asking for books. Then he began to phone people he didn't know throughout Sevier County. The *Ritchfield Reaper,* a weekly newspaper from the town of Ritchfield, wrote about Jason's plans for a library. Soon, the two daily papers in Salt Lake City wrote stories about Jason wanting books. One of the headlines read,

Young Librarian Opens Library—Needs Books!

Jason had to work hard to get his library books organized.

People mailed boxes of books to Jason's home. "Awesome! Where am I going to fit all these books?" Jason said, grinning. He knew that before long he would have enough books to open his library.

Jason, his older sister and brother, and his parents spent two months cleaning out the town hall basement and putting books on shelves. Jason arranged the books in a system so people could find what they wanted easily. His friends and their parents also came to help.

Jason's mother and friends helped, too.

The library opened on Election Day, November 4, 1980. Almost one hundred people came to see the new library. Jason was so tickled. His best friend Dennis Jensen helped Jason in the library after school. In the first year, Elsinore library had about one thousand books. It was a very busy place.

Soon worldwide newspapers wrote articles about Jason's new library. Jason appeared on various television shows, including *Good Morning, America*, *Fantasy*, *The Phil Donahue Show*, and even *The Tonight Show*. On *The Tonight Show*, Johnny Carson asked Jason if there were anything his parents didn't want him to say on television. Jason hesitated, then responded, "They told me not to ask for any more books." More bags full of books flooded Elsinore after the show.

At age eleven, Jason spoke at a joint congressional hearing in Washington, D.C., about the rural needs of America. "Why should I suffer because I live in Elsinore without a library? Salt Lake City has plenty of libraries. Why should my friends suffer?" he asked the joint panel.

Jason went to the White House two times to talk to President Ronald Reagan. *Reading Rainbow* filmed Jason in his library to encourage children to read books in the summer months. *Reader's Digest* wrote a story about Jason.

Jason meets President Ronald Reagan.

Here, Jason sits in his library enjoying a good book.

Jason is a bit embarrassed about all the fuss made over him. He just did what he thought was needed in Elsinore. His library today has sixteen thousand books and occupies two rooms in the town hall basement.

Jason, now eighteen years old, will soon go away to college. He and the council have discussed the future of the library. It will continue to stay open for others who want a library in Elsinore.

◆ LIBRARY LINK ◆

If you enjoyed this selection and would like to read something else about young people doing things on their own, read Summer Business *by Charles Martin.*

Reader's Response

What would you like very much to make happen that would help others?

Jason
Wants a Library

 ### Thinking It Over

1. Why did Jason ride his bicycle six miles to another town?
2. How did Jason plan to run the library?
3. Why do you think the town council finally said yes to Jason's plan?
4. How did the other people in Elsinore feel about having their own library? Explain.
5. What kind of person was Jason? What leads you to describe him this way?
6. What might Jason have done if the town council had said no to his plan?

 ### Writing to Learn

THINK AND DECIDE Jason loves to read good books. Think of three books that you would recommend to him. List the book titles on a sheet of paper.

WRITE Choose one book from your list. Write a letter to Jason telling why you think he would enjoy it.

Making a Character Map

How can you understand the characters you meet in your reading? One good way is to make a character map.

Learning the Strategy

Here are the directions for making a character map.

1. Read the story.
2. Draw a simple picture of the character.
3. Near the picture make four or five lines for writing what the character does or says.
4. Make a long line beneath the picture for writing a sentence that tells what kind of person the character is.

Using the Strategy

Look at the character map for Jason Hardman, who started the library in Elsinore, Utah. The picture shows Jason. The sentences on the lines near his picture tell what he did. At the bottom of the map is the sentence that tells what kind of person Jason was.

He kept calling the mayor.

He was a good talker.

He thought of using the basement.

He worked hard.

He was a good problem solver.

Practice making a character map. On your own paper, copy this map about Jason. Add more things he did and said.

Does the sentence at the bottom tell what kind of person Jason was? You may change the sentence if you want to.

Applying the Strategy to the Next Story

The next story, "The Recital," is about two sisters. As you read, you can make a character map about one of the sisters.

The writing connection can be found on page 233.

THE RECITAL

Maria and Sonia like to do different things—but they meet similar problems.

by Johanna Hurwitz

Anyone who saw Sonia and Maria Torres (tō′ res) together knew they were sisters. Both girls had long, dark hair and the same bright, brown eyes. When they smiled, they both had dimples in their cheeks.

Although the sisters looked alike, they were very different. Maria took piano lessons and loved making music. Sonia loved music, too, but she loved sports even more. Sonia was one of the best players on the girls' soccer team at school. ❖

One hot afternoon after soccer practice, Sonia carefully opened the front door to her house. She could hear Maria playing music, and she didn't want to bother her. Quietly, Sonia walked into the kitchen and opened the refrigerator to get a glass of orange juice.

❖
Make a character map for Maria. Add this information to the map.

196

197

"Get a glass of juice for me, too," said Maria as she came into the kitchen.

"Did I make too much noise?" asked Sonia. "Sorry."

"You weren't noisy," said Maria. "I've been practicing all afternoon for Mrs. Howard's recital, and I was getting ready to take a break."

Sonia nodded her head. It was a real honor to be asked to play in Mrs. Howard's recital, and Maria had been taking lessons for only two years. Most of the students who would be playing had been studying with Mrs. Howard for four or five years. ◆◇◆

◆◇◆
Add this information to Maria's character map.

"I bet you're one of Mrs. Howard's best students," said Sonia.

"I know I play well when I'm at home," Maria said, "but I'm scared to go on stage. What if I make some awful mistakes?"

Sonia gave Maria a hug. "Don't be afraid," she said. "Just relax and pretend you're playing at home and that no one is listening but me."

"I'll try," Maria said.

Two weeks later the recital took place. That morning when she awoke, Maria said that her stomach hurt.

"You're probably just nervous," said Mrs. Torres.

"You should go running with me," said Sonia.

"Running?" said Maria. "You're the runner, not me."

"I know," laughed Sonia. "But if you run with me, it'll help you relax."

"It can't hurt," said Mrs. Torres.

The two sisters ran around the block three times. Sonia ran slowly so that her sister could keep up with her.

"Don't you feel better already?" Sonia asked. "Coach Reynolds says that lively movement, such as running, clears the head."

"What does she say about making mistakes at a recital?" asked Maria.

"She says that if you make a mistake, you just concentrate harder and keep on going. Don't forget the terrible mistake I made in the first game my team played this year," Sonia said.

"What was that?" asked Maria. "I don't remember."

"I kicked the ball in the wrong direction and made a goal for the other team. I was so embarrassed. Imagine helping the other team score! It was awful."

"What did your coach say?" asked Maria.

"She said to concentrate on the next goal and not to look back on the past," Maria answered. "You know, she was right. I concentrated on the game, and I didn't think about what had already happened. Before long, I scored a goal for our team."

The girls ran back to the house. Maria was out of breath from her run, but her stomach no longer hurt. They showered and dressed for the recital.

At the front of the recital hall there was a sign showing the way to the room for Mrs. Howard's recital. The room was large, and there seemed to be over a hundred chairs lined up for the audience.

Maria was beginning to look pale and frightened. Sonia squeezed her sister's hand.

Add this information to Maria's character map.

"Good luck," Sonia whispered to Maria.

Mrs. Howard got up in front of the audience and announced the name of the first student. He looked old enough to be in high school. Sonia watched as he walked stiffly toward the piano. He had black hair, and his face had turned bright red. He looked nervous, too.

The piece that the young man played was one that Sonia had heard Maria practicing at home a long time ago. He played it faster than Maria did. When he was finished, everyone clapped politely.

The next student was a grown woman. She played her piece very slowly, as if she were being extra careful not to make any mistakes. Again, the audience clapped when she finished playing.

Sonia took a deep breath. She listened as Mrs. Howard announced Maria's name and watched her sister as she slowly made her way towards the piano.

Maria sat down on the piano bench with her hands in her lap. Everyone waited for her to begin.

Maria played the opening notes of her piece, but then she made a mistake and stopped. For a moment it looked as if she were going to run off the stage. Sonia held her breath as she looked at her sister. Maria was sitting very stiffly. "You can do it. You can do it," Sonia whispered to herself, wishing that Maria could hear her. She knew how Maria was feeling. Then Maria took a deep breath. She bent toward the keyboard and started again from the beginning of her piece.

Sonia sat back in her chair to listen. The air was filled with the most wonderful sounds. If Maria was still nervous, you could not hear it in her music.

When the music ended, the audience clapped loudly. Everyone could tell that Maria had real talent. The other students had played the notes, but Maria had played music. ◈◈◈

After the recital was over, Mrs. Howard shook hands with Mr. and Mrs. Torres. "Maria is my prize student," she said, hugging Maria. "I know you are proud of her."

◈◈◈
Add this information to Maria's character map.

Maria stood next to Sonia. "I couldn't have done it without your help," she whispered.

"What did I do?" asked Sonia.

"I was going to run off the stage after I made that first mistake, but then I remembered what you told me about soccer. You said that concentrating was the most important thing, and you said not to look back. So I started over, and if I made a little mistake, I just kept on going. I didn't let it upset me."

Sonia was amazed. "I can't believe that tips for playing soccer would be useful for playing the piano!" she laughed.

"Do you have any piano tips to help me play soccer?" Sonia asked Maria. It was something to look into. ◀◆▶

Write a sentence below the character map that describes Maria.

◆ LIBRARY LINK ◆

If you enjoyed this story by Johanna Hurwitz, you might enjoy reading her other books, such as Aldo Applesauce, Aldo Ice Cream, Class Clown, *and* Yellow Blue Jay.

Reader's Response

Have you ever felt the way Maria did before the recital? If so, how did you deal with it?

THE RECITAL

Thinking It Over

1. What was Maria worried about?
2. Why did Sonia take Maria running the morning of the recital?
3. In what way was Maria's recital like Sonia's first soccer game of the year?
4. Why did Sonia remember the mistake she made during the soccer game, while Maria did not remember it? How did you decide on your answer?
5. How did Sonia's advice help Maria?
6. If Maria had not talked to Sonia about her feelings, what might have happened during the recital?

Writing to Learn

THINK AND COMPARE   Maria was worried about being in a recital. Copy the chart below. Finish it with words that tell how Maria felt after the recital was over.

Before	After
• anxious	
• worried	
• tense	
• nervous	
• afraid	

WRITE   Use the words on your chart to help you write a paragraph. Tell how Maria felt after the recital.

Lee Bennett Hopkins
INTERVIEWS

Johanna Hurwitz

Johanna Hurwitz always knew she would be a writer.

"When I was about eight or nine years old, I made up stories to tell to my younger brother," she says. "I started writing them down. I even sent some to children's magazines."

At the age of ten, she wrote and published her first poem, titled "Books." It was about what books meant to her. Mrs. Hurwitz was paid fifty cents for the poem. The fifty cents was sent to her by check!

Mrs. Hurwitz was born and raised in the Bronx, in New York City. "My home was filled with books," she says. "Some of my happiest early memories were when my father and mother read to me. I lived in a neighborhood that was filled with children. I could walk to the library, and I did so almost every day. The library was my other home. I loved it so much that I decided by the age of ten that someday I would become a librarian. I also knew then that I would one day write books."

In high school, Mrs. Hurwitz started working in a public library. After graduating from college, she became a full-time children's librarian.

She still finds time from her busy writing schedule to work part-time as a children's librarian at the Great Neck Library in Great Neck, New York. There she reads to children and tells them stories. "I'll never stop working in libraries," she says. "I love it so much."

Mrs. Hurwitz and her husband, Uri, a teacher and writer, have two grown children, Nomi and Beni. She made up stories to tell to her children when they were young. It was not until they were in school that she began to write the stories down.

Her first book, *Busybody Nora*, a story about a six-year-old girl who lives in an apartment in New York City, was published in 1976. Since then she has written almost twenty books.

"My ideas come from everywhere—from my own children, and from children I meet and work with when I visit schools and libraries," she says. "Sometimes, something that someone says, or something that I see on the street or on television will give me an idea.

"When I am not writing, I like to cook and listen to music. Both food and music have crept into several of my books. In *Busybody Nora*, the folk tales *Jack and the Beanstalk* and *Stone Soup* play an important part in the book." Food has also crept into some of the titles of her books, such as *Aldo Ice Cream* and *Aldo Applesauce*.

Another favorite hobby she enjoys is baseball. "I'm a baseball fanatic," she says. Her book *Baseball Fever* came about because of her love of the sport. "I grew up near New York's Yankee Stadium," she says. "I could hear the fans' screaming and cheering coming from the stadium every time a player hit a home run. Loving baseball as I do, it was natural for me to write *Baseball Fever*. I've got it!"

I asked Mrs. Hurwitz if she had any advice to give to young writers. "Yes," she said. "I would like boys and girls to know that writing does not come easily. If you want to be a good baseball player or a fine ballet dancer, you must practice, practice, practice. To become a fine writer, you must practice, also.

"Reading is very important, too. If you want to become a writer, read a lot. The more you read, the larger your vocabulary becomes. Also, the more you read, the more you become aware of how a story really works."

The story you have just read, "The Recital," was written by Mrs. Hurwitz especially for this book.

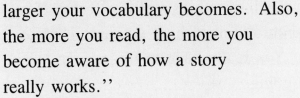

"Like most stories," she says, "it was made up. When I was a young girl, though, I did take piano lessons, and I did not like playing in front of people."

In "The Recital," Maria's sister tells her to concentrate on the next goal and not to look back at mistakes. "Writers should also remember not to look back at mistakes," she says. "If baseball players make mistakes in games and keep thinking about the mistakes, the rest of the game will not go as well for them. You should just think about the next thing you are going to do—as Maria did. You really have to forget past mistakes and keep going.

"Whatever you do in life, believe in yourself. Don't give up. Keep plugging away. Whether you are running in a marathon race, or creating a piece of artwork, or writing a poem, story, or a report, stay with it. Believe in it."

Reader's Response

How do you feel about Johanna Hurwitz's advice, "Believe in yourself. Don't give up"?

LEE BENNETT HOPKINS INTERVIEWS
Johanna Hurwitz

Thinking It Over

1. How might Johanna Hurwitz's happy childhood have led her to become a writer? What makes you think this?
2. List the things Johanna Hurwitz does that show she still loves books.
3. What are some of Johanna Hurwitz's other interests?
4. Where does Johanna Hurwitz get her ideas for stories?
5. Explain what you think Mrs. Hurwitz meant when she said, "The more you read, the more you become aware of how a story really works." Do you agree?

Writing to Learn

THINK AND RECALL   Mrs. Hurwitz says, "Whatever you do in life, believe in yourself. Don't give up. Keep plugging away." What advice would you give a younger child?

WRITE   Share your ideas with a younger friend. Write a letter and give advice that you believe in.

211

LITERATURE LINK

Why is the story setting important?

In "The Recital," you read about the place where Maria's recital was held.

> At the front of the recital hall there was a sign showing the way to the room for Mrs. Howard's recital. The room was large, and there seemed to be over a hundred chairs lined up for the audience.

Can you imagine how Maria felt as she waited to play the piano in front of so many people in such a large room? If so, you know why this setting is important to the story.

When and Where

The setting of a story is where and when the story takes place. Sometimes stories happen in places you know. Other times, they happen in faraway or make-believe lands. Stories can take place long ago, today, or many years from now.

An author may use words alone or add pictures to help you see the setting in your mind. Picturing the setting can make you feel like you are there. You can understand, for example, why playing in a recital hall made Maria nervous.

You will enjoy the story more if you picture where and when it is happening. So, try keeping the setting in mind as you read.

As you read "A Day When Frogs Wear Shoes," ask yourself where and when the story takes place. Then put yourself in the story to make the time and place seem real.

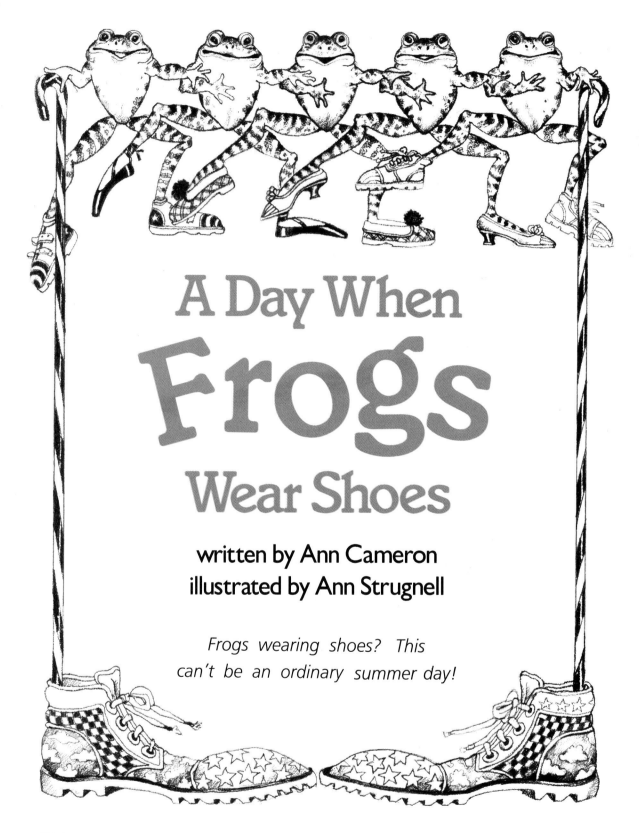

A Day When
Frogs
Wear Shoes

written by Ann Cameron
illustrated by Ann Strugnell

Frogs wearing shoes? This can't be an ordinary summer day!

My little brother, Huey, my best friend, Gloria, and I were sitting on our front steps. It was one of those hot summer days when everything stands still. We didn't know what to do. We were watching the grass grow. It didn't grow fast.

"You know something?" Gloria said. "This is a slow day."

"It's so slow the dogs don't bark," Huey said.

"It's so slow the flies don't fly," Gloria said.

"It's so slow ice cream wouldn't melt," I said.

"If we had any ice cream," Huey said.

"But we don't," Gloria said.

We watched the grass some more.

"We better do something," I said.

"Like what?" Gloria asked.

"We could go visit Dad," Huey said.

"That's a terrible idea," I said.

"Why?" Huey asked. "I like visiting Dad."

My father has a shop about a mile from our house, where he fixes cars. Usually it is fun to visit him. If he has customers, he always introduces us as if we were important guests. Sometimes he buys us treats.

"Huey," I said, "usually, visiting Dad is a good idea. Today, it's an especially dangerous idea."

"Why?" Gloria said.

"Because we're bored," I said. "My dad hates it when people are bored. He says the world is so interesting nobody should ever be bored."

"I see," Gloria said, as if she didn't.

"So we'll go see him," Huey said, "and we just won't tell him we're bored. We're bored, but we won't tell him."

"Just so you remember that!" I said.

"Oh, I'll remember," Huey said.

Huey was wearing his angel look. When he has that look, you know he'll never remember anything.

Huey and I put on sweat bands. Gloria put on dark glasses. We started out.

The sun shined up at us from the sidewalks. Even the shadows on the street were hot as blankets.

Huey picked up a stick and scratched it along the sidewalk. "Oh, we're bored," he muttered. "Bored, bored, bored, bored, bored!"

"Huey!" I yelled. I wasn't bored anymore. I was nervous.

Finally we reached a sign that read, "Ralph's Car Hospital."

That's my dad's sign. My dad is Ralph.

The parking lot had three cars in it. Dad was inside the shop, lifting the hood of another car. He didn't have any customers with him, so we didn't get to shake hands and feel like visiting mayors or congressmen.

"Hi, Dad," I said.

RALPH'S CAR HOSPITAL

Punctures
Rust
Dents & Bashes
Bad Brakes
Bad Breaks
Unusual Complaints

"Hi!" my dad said.

"We're—" Huey said.

I didn't trust Huey. I stepped on his foot.

"We're on a hike," I said.

"Well, nice of you to stop by," my father said. "If you want, you can stay a while and help me."

"OK," we said.

So Huey sorted nuts and bolts. Gloria shined fenders with a rag. I held a new windshield wiper while my dad put it on a car window.

"Nice work, Huey and Julian and Gloria!" my dad said when we were done.

And then he sent us to the store across the street to buy paper cups and ice cubes and a can of frozen lemonade.

We mixed the lemonade in the shop. Then we sat out under the one tree by the side of the driveway and drank all of it.

"Good lemonade!" my father said. "So what are you kids going to do now?"

"Oh, hike!" I reminded him.

"You know," my father answered, "I'm surprised at you kids picking a hot day like today for a hike. The ground is so hot. On a day like this, frogs wear shoes!"

"They do?" Huey said.

"Especially if they go hiking," my father said. "Of course, a lot of frogs, on a day like this, would stay home. So I wonder why you kids are hiking."

Sometimes my father notices too much. Then he gets yellow lights shining in his eyes, asking you to tell the whole truth. That's when I know to look at my feet.

"Oh," I said, "we like hiking."

But Gloria didn't know any better. She looked into my father's eyes. "Really," she said, "this wasn't a real hike. We came to see you."

"Oh, I see!" my father said, looking pleased.

"Because we were bored," Huey said.

My father jumped up so fast he tipped over his lemonade cup. "BORED!" my father yelled. "You were BORED?"

He picked up his cup and waved it in the air. "And you think I don't get BORED?" my father roared, sprinkling out a few last drops of lemonade from his cup. "You think I don't get bored fixing cars when it's hot enough that frogs wear shoes?"

"'This is such an interesting world that nobody should ever be bored.' That's what you said," I reminded him.

"Last week," Huey added.

"Ummm," my father said. He got quiet.

He rubbed his hand over his mouth, the way he does when he's thinking.

"Why, of course," my father said, "I remember that. And it's the perfect, absolute truth. People absolutely SHOULD NOT get bored! However —" He paused. "It just happens that, sometimes, they do."

My father rubbed a line in the dirt with his shoe. He was thinking so hard I could see his thoughts standing by the tree and sitting on all the fenders of the cars.

"You know, if you three would kindly help me some more, I could leave a half hour early, and we could drive down by the river."

"We'll help," I said.

"Yes, and then we can look for frogs!" Huey said.
So we stayed. We learned how to make a signal light
blink. And afterward, on the way to the river, my
dad bought us all ice cream cones. The ice cream did
melt. Huey's melted all down the front of his shirt. It
took him ten paper napkins and the river to clean up.

After Huey's shirt was clean, we took our shoes and socks off and went wading. We looked for special rocks under the water—the ones that are beautiful until you take them out of the water, when they get dry and not so bright.

We found skipping stones and tried to see who could get the most skips from a stone.

We saw a school of minnows going as fast as they could to get away from us.

But we didn't see any frogs.

"If you want to see frogs," my father said, "you'll have to walk down the bank a ways and look hard."

So we decided to do that.

"Fine!" my father said. "But I'll stay here. I think I'm ready for a little nap."

"Naps are boring!" we said.

"Sometimes it's nice to be bored," my father said.

We left him with his eyes closed, sitting under a tree.

Huey saw the first frog. He almost stepped on it. It jumped into the water, and we ran after it.

Huey caught it and picked it up, and then I saw another one. I grabbed it.

It was slippery and strong and its body was cold, just like it wasn't the middle of summer.

Then Gloria caught one, too. The frogs wriggled in our hands, and we felt their hearts beating. Huey looked at their funny webbed feet.

"Their feet are good for swimming," he said, "but Dad is wrong. They don't wear shoes!"

"No way," Gloria said. "They sure don't wear shoes."

"Let's go tell him," I said.

We threw our frogs back into the river. They made little trails swimming away from us. And then we went back to my father. He was sitting under the tree with his eyes shut. It looked like he hadn't moved an inch.

"We found frogs," Huey said, "and we've got news for you. They don't wear shoes!"

My father's eyes opened. "They don't?" he said. "Well, I can't be right about everything. Dry your feet. Put your shoes on. It's time to go."

We all sat down to put on our shoes.

I pulled out a sock and put it on.

I stuck my foot into my shoe. My foot wouldn't go in. I picked up the shoe and looked inside.

"Oh no!" I yelled.

There were two little eyes inside my shoe, looking out at me. Huey and Gloria grabbed their socks. All our shoes had frogs in them, every one.

"What did I tell you," my father said.

"You were right," we said. "It's a day when frogs wear shoes!"

◆ LIBRARY LINK ◆

This story was taken from the book More Stories Julian Tells *by Ann Cameron. You might enjoy reading the entire book to find out more about Julian, Gloria, and Huey.*

 Reader's Response

Do you think Julian's father was right in saying nobody should ever be bored? Explain your answer.

A Day When Frogs Wear Shoes

Thinking It Over

1. Why couldn't Julian, Huey, and Gloria find anything to do?
2. Why did the children visit Julian's dad in his shop?
3. Did Julian's dad understand how the children were feeling? How do you know?
4. Do you think the children believed they would find frogs wearing shoes? Tell why or why not.
5. How did the frogs get into the children's shoes?
6. What are some examples of figurative language in the story?

Writing to Learn

THINK AND INVENT   Riddles are fun. A character riddle gives clues about a person. Read the riddle below.

Character Riddle

I am always first to arrive at school.
I work hard every day.
I like children.
Who am I?

(Our teacher.)

WRITE   Make up a character riddle about someone you know. See if others can guess who your riddle is about.

225

Phillis Wheatley was one of America's first poets. Her life story is like no other person's that you will ever read about.

Phillis Wheatley

America's First Black Poet

by Kacey Brown

Many, many years ago, a young girl arrived in Boston, Massachusetts. The year was 1761. It was not by choice that she was making the long voyage. She had been taken from a small village in Africa and put aboard a slave ship heading for Boston Harbor.

The young girl was not happy to be in Boston. The voyage from Africa had been long and difficult. She was alone, separated from her family and friends. She was sad, but she had a quiet gentleness about her. She was determined to make the best of her difficult situation.

As soon as the slave ship docked in Boston Harbor, this young girl and the other Africans on the ship were sold. The girl was lucky because John Wheatley, a wealthy tailor, bought her. He was a kind man who wanted a servant for his wife Susannah. He thought the quiet child was a good choice.

Early Days at the Wheatleys

The Wheatleys named the young girl Phillis. Phillis could not speak English, so she couldn't tell the Wheatleys anything about herself. They guessed that she was between seven and eight years old. They thought that because some of her baby teeth were missing.

Phillis was a bright child who learned things quickly. Her bright mind and gentle ways made the Wheatleys very fond of her. They did not treat her like the other slaves in their house. Phillis was treated like one of the family. She was given her own room and ate her meals with the family. Phillis was asked to do only a few easy chores around the house. Before long, the Wheatleys began to think of her as a daughter.

The Wheatleys had two children, Mary and Nathaniel. They were twins who were about ten years older than Phillis. Mary enjoyed spending time with Phillis. When they were together, she taught Phillis to speak English. In a very short time, Phillis learned to read and write, too. In only sixteen months from the time she had arrived in Boston, Phillis was able to read and understand even the most difficult parts of the Bible. This amazed the Wheatleys. Phillis had learned to read and write at a time when few children her age could read and fewer still could write. Phillis's love for reading continued throughout her life.

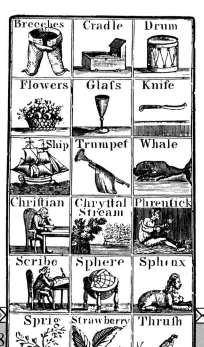

This page is from an 18th century schoolbook.

228

Poet at Age Thirteen

Because of her love of reading, Phillis continued to write, too. In 1766, when Phillis was only thirteen years old, she wrote the first of her many poems. Then, in 1770, she wrote a poem in honor of a local minister, George Whitefield. It was printed in a Boston newspaper. The sale of that poem was the beginning of her career as a poet. People throughout the Boston area enjoyed reading her poetry.

Soon Phillis was known as an excellent writer. The people who visited the Wheatleys were eager to meet the young black poet. Phillis was also invited to the homes of many of the citizens of Boston. She even wrote poems for some of them.

Phillis loved to write as much as she loved to read. She was always thinking of ways to write about the things she read. Sometimes Phillis got ideas for her poetry late at night, so she kept a pen and paper next to her bed. Then, if she awakened during the night with a good idea for a poem, she would light the candle next to her bed and write her thoughts on a piece of paper.

Phillis's Fame Grows

As more and more people in Boston read her poems, Phillis's fame grew. Her charm and pleasant company made her even more popular. When newspapers from Boston reached England, people there read her poems. The Countess of Huntingdon, an English woman who was related to the king of England, helped to make Phillis's poetry popular in England. The countess enjoyed reading Phillis's poem about George Whitefield so much that she had it printed in England. During this time, the countess and Phillis began writing letters to one another and a friendship between them grew.

Things were going well for Phillis. Then, in 1773, she became ill. The Wheatleys were very worried about her. Their family doctor thought that a sea voyage would help her recover. So Nathaniel took Phillis on a voyage to England. When the Countess of Huntingdon heard they were coming to England, she invited Phillis and Nathaniel to stay with her. While they were in England, the countess made arrangements to have Phillis's poems printed in a book. People in England began to talk about Phillis's poetry, and her popularity grew.

Phillis was only in England five weeks when she received a letter from Mr. Wheatley with the sad news that Mrs. Wheatley was very ill. Immediately Phillis made plans to return to Boston. She wanted to get back to Boston as soon as she could so that she could be with Mrs. Wheatley. Phillis did get back in time to see Mrs. Wheatley, who died a short time later. Mr. Wheatley died soon after. Even though these events caused great sadness for Phillis, she continued to write. Now she was writing not only for herself but also for the Wheatleys, who had helped her so much.

Phillis Meets George Washington

A few months after Phillis returned to Boston, America began its war against England. Americans wanted to be free from England's rule. To prepare for the war, General George Washington went to Cambridge, Massachusetts, as head of the American army. It was an exciting time for people in the Boston area! They were eager to meet the man who would lead them in their struggle for freedom. Phillis had heard about General Washington. She knew that he was a great man.

The following year she wrote a letter to General Washington to wish him success. In her letter, she included a poem she had written about him. Part of the poem read:

Thee, first in peace and honours . . .
Fam'd for thy valour, for thy virtues
more. . . .

General Washington was so pleased with the poem that he sent Phillis a personal thank-you note and invited her to visit him in Cambridge, Massachusetts. Phillis was delighted.

Phillis Wheatley, the shy young girl who came to Boston as a slave in 1761, met and talked to the man who would become the first president of the United States. She had come to Boston unable to read or write and later went on to become a well-known poet. Phillis Wheatley's poetry is an example of what a young person can accomplish on her own.

 Reader's Response

If you could talk to Phillis Wheatley what questions would you ask her?

Phillis Wheatley
America's First Black Poet

Thinking It Over

1. How did Phillis Wheatley come to America?
2. What was special about the way in which the Wheatleys treated Phillis?
3. How did learning to read and write change Phillis Wheatley's life?
4. Do you think Phillis Wheatley's life was unusual? What led you to your answer?

Writing to Learn

THINK AND DESCRIBE   Can you make a character map of Phillis Wheatley? Think about what she was like and the things she did. Then, on your paper, complete the character map of her.

Phillis had a will to learn.

Phillis Wheatley

WRITE   Write sentences that tell what kind of person Phillis Wheatley was.

NARCISSA

Some of the girls are playing jacks.
Some are playing ball.
But small Narcissa is not playing
Anything at all.

Small Narcissa sits upon
A brick in her back yard
And looks at tiger lilies,
And shakes her pigtails hard.

First she is an ancient queen
In pomp and purple veil.
Soon she is a singing wind.
And, next, a nightingale.

How fine to be Narcissa,
A-changing like all that!
While sitting still, as still, as still
As anyone ever sat!

Gwendolyn Brooks

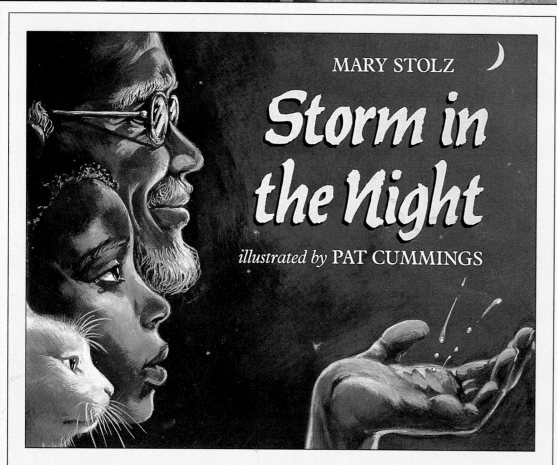

MARY STOLZ

Storm in the Night

illustrated by PAT CUMMINGS

Grandfather and Thomas sat on the swing, creaking back and forth, back and forth, as thunder boomed and lightning stabbed across the sky. from *Storm in the Night* by Mary Stolz

What would you do if the lights went out during a bad thunderstorm? Would you crawl under your bed and hide? You certainly wouldn't be able to watch television, and if the storm was at night, it would be too dark to read a book.

In *Storm in the Night*, Thomas and Grandfather plan to have a quiet evening, reading and watching television. But then a terrible thunderstorm hits, and the power goes out. It is dark and very stormy. Wind and rain toss the trees to and fro, thunder crashes loudly, and lightning splits the night sky. Even poor Ringo the cat shivers. There will be no television or books this night, and it is too early to go to bed.

If you read *Storm in the Night*, you will find out what Thomas and Grandfather do when the lights go out. Maybe you will get an idea of what *you* can do the next time a thunderstorm changes *your* plans.

Alexander

Horrible, No Good,

and the Terrible, Very Bad Day

written by Judith Viorst
illustrated by Ray Cruz

We all have days when everything seems to go wrong. But wait until you hear what happens to Alexander!

I went to sleep with gum in my mouth and now there's gum in my hair and when I got out of bed this morning I tripped on the skateboard and by mistake I dropped my sweater in the sink while the water was running and I could tell it was going to be a terrible, horrible, no good, very bad day.

At breakfast Anthony found a Corvette Sting Ray car kit in his breakfast cereal box and Nick found a Junior Undercover Agent code ring in his breakfast cereal box but in my breakfast cereal box all I found was breakfast cereal.

I think I'll move to Australia.

In the car pool Mrs. Gibson let Becky have a seat by the window. Audrey and Elliott got seats by the window too. I said I was being scrunched. I said I was being smushed. I said, if I don't get a seat by the window I am going to be carsick. No one even answered.

I could tell it was going to be a terrible, horrible, no good, very bad day.

At school Mrs. Dickens liked Paul's picture of the sailboat better than my picture of the invisible castle.

At singing time she said I sang too loud. At counting time she said I left out sixteen. Who needs sixteen?

I could tell it was going to be a terrible, horrible, no good, very bad day.

I could tell because Paul said I wasn't his best friend anymore. He said that Philip Parker was his best friend and that Albert Moyo was his next best friend and that I was only his third best friend.

I hope you sit on a tack, I said to Paul. I hope the next time you get a double-decker strawberry ice-cream cone the ice cream part falls off the cone part and lands in Australia.

There were two cupcakes in Philip Parker's lunch bag and Albert got a Hershey bar with almonds and Paul's mother gave him a piece of jelly roll that had little coconut sprinkles on the top. Guess whose mother forgot to put in dessert?

It was a terrible, horrible, no good, very bad day.

That's what it was, because after school my mom took us all to the dentist and Dr. Fields found a cavity just in me. Come back next week and I'll fix it, said Dr. Fields.

Next week, I said, I'm going to Australia.

On the way downstairs the elevator door closed on my foot and while we were waiting for my mom to go get the car Anthony made me fall where it was muddy and then when I started crying because of the mud Nick said I was a crybaby and while I was punching Nick for saying crybaby my mom came back with the car and scolded me for being muddy and fighting.

I am having a terrible, horrible, no good, very bad day, I told everybody. No one even answered.

So then we went to the shoestore to buy some sneakers. Anthony chose white ones with blue stripes. Nick chose red ones with white stripes. I chose blue ones with red stripes but then the shoe man said, We're all sold out. They made me buy plain old white ones, but they can't make me wear them.

When we picked up my dad at his office he said
I couldn't play with his copying machine, but I forgot.
He also said to watch out for the books on his desk,
and I was careful as could be except for my elbow.
He also said don't fool around with his phone, but I
think I called Australia. My dad said please don't pick
him up anymore.

It was a terrible, horrible, no good, very bad day.

There were lima beans for dinner and I hate limas.

There was kissing on TV and I hate kissing.

My bath was too hot, I got soap in my eyes, my marble went down the drain, and I had to wear my railroad-train pajamas. I hate my railroad-train pajamas.

When I went to bed Nick took back the pillow he said I could keep and the Mickey Mouse night light burned out and I bit my tongue.

The cat wants to sleep with Anthony, not with me.

It has been a terrible, horrible, no good, very bad day.

My mom says some days are like that.

Even in Australia.

◆ LIBRARY LINK ◆

If you enjoyed this story by Judith Viorst, you might enjoy reading some poems from her book, If I Were in Charge of the World and Other Worries.

 Reader's Response

Do you think that Alexander really wanted to move to Australia? Have you ever felt the way he did? Explain your answers.

WRITING ABOUT READING

Writing a Helpful Note

Many of the characters that you read about in this unit had problems to solve. For example, Maria was nervous about her recital. Her sister found a way to help her.

Imagine that you are able to help a character from one of the stories in this unit. What could you do to help? You can write a note telling what you would do.

Prewriting

Choose a story character from this unit whose problem is interesting to you. Reread the story in which that character appears. Think about what you could do to help. This diagram may help you plan.

Helping Hands	
Name of Character	
Character's Problem	
What I Might Do To Help	

Writing

Begin your note with a greeting such as "Dear Julian." Explain to the character your view of the problem. Then write what you could do to help. Tell as clearly as you can *how* you would put your idea into action. Explain why you think you have a good idea.

Revising

Read your note to a partner. Ask your partner if you have explained your ideas clearly. Be sure that all the words tell exactly what you mean. If some words don't, think of other words that explain your ideas more clearly.

Proofreading

Use a dictionary to check your spelling. Make sure you have used periods and commas correctly. Then make a clean copy of your note.

Publishing

Use the notes to create a class newspaper column called "Helping Hands."

Making a Story Mobile

Lemonade, a hot sun, frogs, and shoes are all part of the story "A Day When Frogs Wear Shoes."

Today, you and your classmates will make a mobile about a story in this unit.

Before you begin, decide who will be responsible for one or more of these jobs:

◆ Encouraging everyone to share ideas

◆ Making sure everyone understands the directions

◆ Showing appreciation for people's ideas

◆ Recording everyone's ideas on a list

Start by asking someone in the group to gather the materials you will need. Then, together discuss the stories in this unit and choose one for your mobile. Take turns suggesting objects that are important in the story. Make a list of everyone's ideas. Next, each person will draw one of the objects and cut it out. Finally, everyone will help put the mobile together by hanging the pictures from a stick or hanger.

Ask your friends to guess which story your mobile is about.

The Courage of Sarah Noble by Alice Dalgliesh *(Scribner, 1952)* In 1707, a girl helps her father build a log house in the wilderness. When her father sets off to get the rest of the family, Sarah is left to deal with the wilderness alone.

Anna, Grandpa, and the Big Storm by Carla Stevens *(Houghton Mifflin, 1982)* During the great blizzard of 1888 in New York City, Anna is determined to go to the final round of the spelling bee. Grandpa offers to go with her.

Chin Chiang and the Dragon's Dance by Ian Wallace *(Atheneum, 1984)* A young boy is old enough to do the New Year's good luck dance. He is afraid he will be clumsy but finds the courage to try.

GET THE MESSAGE

*𝒯alking, writing,
signaling, signing –
why do people
send their
messages in
different ways?*

THE LETTER,
painting by Mary Cassatt, American, 1891

*Some people think predicting
the weather is a tough job. Others
think it's a guessing game.*

FORECAST

written by Malcolm Hall
illustrated by Bruce Degen

"Speech! Speech!" the animals chanted. Theodore Cat smiled and stood up.

"Well, if you insist," he said.

"We didn't mean *you,* Theodore," groaned the animals. "We want a speech from Stan!"

"Oh, *him,*" said Theodore.

Stan Groundhog stood up. He looked around shyly. The whole party was in his honor. After twenty years, Stan was retiring. He was leaving his job as weather forecaster for the *Claws and Paws* newspaper. "I can't think of anything to say," said Stan.

"Then make a forecast!" yelled Humphrey Snake from the back of the room.

"What a good idea," said Theodore, who was the editor of the paper and the boss of all the animals. "Stan, give us your last official weather prediction."

"Well—okay," said Stan. He went to the window and peeked outside; next he looked down at his shadow, then he sighed. "I predict it will be warm and sunny all afternoon. There is no chance of rain." The animals cheered. "Now I have to be going," said Stan. "Thanks for the party."

Stan put on a raincoat and galoshes. He opened an umbrella.

"Wait a minute," said Oscar Raccoon. "Why are you going out dressed like that? I thought you said it wasn't going to rain."

"If I have learned one thing," said Stan, "it is never take chances."

And with that, a tremendous crack of lightning jumped across the sky! All the lights in the office went out. Rain began to pour down in bucketfuls. "Do you see what I mean?" said Stan. He waved good-bye and left.

The lights flickered a bit and finally came back on. Oscar looked around. "Is everybody okay?" One by one, the animals nodded. Except— where was Theodore? "Theodore!" shouted Oscar. "Where are you?"

"There he is!" shouted Frank Beaver. He pointed to the floor. "I see his tail!"

Theodore's face was red as he crawled out from under the desk. The animals grinned. "I wasn't hiding, if that's what you're all thinking," he snapped. "I was—uh—considering something—that's what I was doing."

"Oh? And what were you considering?" asked Oscar.

Theodore glared. "I was considering that we will need a new forecaster to take Stan's place. So there!" Theodore looked around the room. "Does anyone know a groundhog who needs a job?"

Caroline Porcupine raised her hand. "Does the forecaster *have* to be a groundhog?"

"Of course," said Theodore. "Everyone knows that groundhogs know *whether* or not spring is coming. That's why they make good *whethermen.*" Theodore laughed at what he thought was a very good joke.

Most of the animals, however, moaned.

Caroline went on. "Anyway, Theodore," she said, "I want the job, even if I am not a groundhog. I know a lot about the weather. Last year, I took a class in meteorology."

"Meteorology?" said Humphrey. "What's that mean?"

"Everyone knows that," said Theodore. "Meteorology is the science of meteors. You know, shooting stars."

"It is not!" snapped Caroline. "Meteorology is the science of weather!"

"Is that so?" said Theodore.

"Yes it is," said Caroline right back. "I can make real forecasts—not just guesses like Stan. If you give me a chance, I will prove it."

"Okay," grumbled Theodore. "Let's make a bet. You forecast the weather for all next week. If you are right five days in a row, I will *consider* you for the job. But if you are wrong once, I'll get a groundhog."

"Theodore, I'll take your bet," said Caroline.

The next day, Caroline brought in her weather instruments. All that morning, Caroline set them up. Soon wires and dials were everywhere.

By afternoon she was ready. She looked at the instruments, one after the other. On a pad of paper she wrote down how hot it was, how damp it was, how fast the wind was blowing, and everything else.

Then Caroline picked up the telephone. She called forecasters all over the country. They told her what the weather was like in their towns. Caroline wrote this down, too.

Finally, Caroline put all the numbers on a map. She connected the numbers with lines. Just then Theodore walked up. "Very good," he said. "I have never seen a better drawing of spaghetti!" He laughed and laughed at his own joke.

No one else did, however.

Caroline looked up. "I am ready to make my forecast. Today is Monday. It will be clear for the rest of the day. Tuesday, it will be sunny and warm. Wednesday, it will be windy and cold. Thursday, it will rain."

The animals looked at each other and smiled. So far, the forecast sounded good— maybe Caroline would be right!

Caroline went on. "And last, Friday. It will be cold in the morning, with snow in the afternoon."

Theodore yeowled with laughter. "Snow? Did you say *snow*? Caroline, look outside. It's the middle of summer!"

Caroline folded her arms stubbornly across her chest. "My instruments say it will snow on Friday. Anyway, every now and then it does snow in summer. In July of 1816, for example . . ."

"Okay, okay," said Theodore. "If it snows on Friday, you get the job for sure. But meanwhile, I'm going to keep on looking for a groundhog!"

That afternoon was sunny. The day after that was warm and clear. Caroline had been right.

Wednesday was windy and cold. Caroline had been right again. Everyone clapped her on the back. Except Theodore. He stared gloomily out his window. "She has been right three days in a row," he thought. "That is better than Stan ever did."

Thursday started out rainy and stayed that way the whole day. Theodore tromped in, soaked, as mad and miserable as a wet cat. Again, he thought. "Four days in a row. Maybe I *should* give Caroline the job even if it doesn't snow on Friday."

But then—"Aaaaa—choooo!" Theodore sneezed. Papers flew everywhere.

"Now see what's happened," he snarled. "I have a cold. And it's all Caroline's fault! If she hadn't forecast this rain, it never would have happened!"

That night, Frank and Oscar walked home together. "It's too bad Caroline predicted snow," said Frank. "She really wants that job."

Oscar nodded. "It will never snow tomorrow. Poor Caroline." Then Oscar stopped. He winked at Frank. "Suppose we help the weather a bit? Even if it only snowed a little, Theodore would still have to give Caroline the job."

"What do you have in mind?" asked Frank.

"Come to my house for dinner," said Oscar, "and I will tell you."

Friday started out cold, just as Caroline had predicted. But by noon, there was still no sign of snow. Theodore sat in his office sniffling and looking out the window.

If Theodore had turned his head, he would have seen Frank and Oscar tiptoe past his door. Each one carried a large sack. They were headed for the ladder that went up to the roof.

A few minutes later, Theodore gasped. A white flake had drifted down past his window! Then came another flake . . . and another . . . and another! He jumped up. "Snow! It's really snowing!"

Theodore ran out of his office. "Caroline! Congratulations! It's snowing! You are the greatest forecaster ever! I take back everything I said."

Theodore yelled to Morris Squirrel. "Stop the presses! I want a new headline for our new forecaster: 'CAROLINE EXPECTS SNOW!'"

Theodore was so excited, he nearly hugged Caroline. He remembered just in time that you *never* hug a porcupine.

So instead he dragged Caroline into his office. "See!" He pointed outside at the flakes.

Caroline squinted. "That doesn't look like snow to me," she said.

"Of course it is," said Theodore. He raised
the window. Flakes started to drift in. One
landed on Theodore's nose. "*Aaaa—choo!!!*" For
a moment Theodore looked surprised. Then, he
looked suspicious.

"Snow never tickled before. Let me see that
'snowflake.'" He grabbed the flake and held it
up to the light. "I thought so. This is a
feather!"

Theodore ran to the window. He poked his
head outside and looked up at the roof. There
was Oscar, holding a half-empty pillowcase in
one hand and a handful of feathers in the other.

"Oh! Hello, Theodore. I was just—"

"Come down from there!" roared Theodore.

A few minutes later, Oscar and Caroline
were standing side by side in Theodore's office.
"So! You two thought you could trick me."

"Caroline had nothing to do with this," said
Oscar. "It was all my idea."

"Hah!" Theodore snorted. "I don't believe you, any more than I really believed it was snowing out there." He pointed out the window. Once more, flakes were drifting down.

"What? More feathers? That does it! I suppose Frank's up there, too."

Again Theodore poked his head out the window. But this time, it was *really* snowing. A large, powdery snowball whacked him between the eyes!

"*Whaaag!*" spat Theodore. Then he licked his whiskers. "That's *real* snow!"

"Of course it is," said Caroline. "I told you it would snow."

Just then, Frank came climbing down the ladder from the roof. His brown fur was covered with snow. "Theodore! Caroline! Oscar! Why are you still inside? Come on out!"

And they all did.

◆ LIBRARY LINK ◆

If you liked reading this story by Malcolm Hall, you might enjoy reading another of his books, Headlines.

 Reader's Response

Would you try to help a friend the way Oscar and Frank did? Why or why not?

FORECAST

Thinking It Over

1. Why were the animals having a party?
2. What did you learn about Theodore when you read he had crawled under his desk?
3. Why did Theodore think that a weather forecaster had to be a groundhog?
4. Why was Caroline confident she could do a good job?
5. Do you think the test Theodore gave Caroline was fair? Why? How did you decide on your answer?

Writing to Learn

THINK AND IMAGINE Imagine that you are a weather forecaster. Draw a simple outline of the state where you live. Add symbols to show what the weather is like. Use snowflakes, raindrops, a sun, or clouds (with puffy cheeks for wind). Use numbers to show the temperature.

WRITE Write sentences to describe the weather shown on your map. Is it sunny or cloudy? Is it going to rain or snow? Is it windy? What is the temperature?

Secret Talk

I have a friend
and sometimes we meet
and greet each other
without a word.

We walk through a field
and stalk a bird
and chew a blade of
pungent grass.

264

We let time pass
for a golden hour
while we twirl a flower
of Queen Ann's lace

or find a lion's face
shaped in a cloud
that's drifting, sifting
across the sky.

There's no need to say,
"It's been a fine day"
when we say goodbye:
when we say goodbye
we just wave a hand
and we understand.

Eve Merriam

265

Words In Our Hands

by Ada B. Litchfield

There are many ways to "talk" and to "listen."

My name is Michael Turner. I am nine years old. I have two sisters, Gina and Diane, a dog named Polly, and two parents who can't hear me when I talk.

They never have heard me. You see, my mom and dad were born deaf.

My parents never heard any sounds at all when they were babies. Some people think a person who can't hear can't learn to talk. That's not true.

266

My mom and dad went to a school for deaf
kids when they were growing up. That's where they
learned to talk. They learned by placing their
fingers on their teacher's throat and feeling how
words felt in her voice box as she said them. They
learned how words looked by watching her face,
especially her lips, as she spoke. It's hard to learn
to say words that way. But my parents did.

They don't talk much now, but they can talk.
Their voices are not like other peoples'. My parents
have never heard other people talking or even their
own voices, so they don't know how voices sound.
It's not always easy to understand what they are
saying, but Gina and Diane and I can.

Sometimes my mother and father can understand what people are saying by reading their lips. That's another thing my parents learned at their school—lip reading.

Reading lips is hard. Some people don't move their lips much when they talk, or they hide their mouths with their hands or with a moustache. Besides, many words look alike when you say them. Look in the mirror and say *pin* and *bin, hand* and *and, hill* and *ill.* See what I mean?

How we move our bodies and what our faces look like when we talk help our parents read our lips. But most of the time we talk to them with our hands as well as our mouths. Grandma Ellis says we have words in our hands.

One way to talk with your hands is to learn a special alphabet so you can spell words with your fingers. This is called finger spelling.

Look at this alphabet. Can you finger spell your name?

Another way to hand talk is to use sign language. Once you have learned sign language, it is easier and faster than finger spelling.

Everybody uses sign language. You can tell your friends to "go away" without using your voice. But sign language for the deaf is like French or Spanish. You have to learn many signs that other people understand before you can talk to anybody.

American Manual Alphabet

Gina, Diane, and I are learning new signs all the time. My mother and father learned sign language when they were little. They taught us signs when we were babies, just as hearing parents teach their children words. Our grandparents, friends, and neighbors helped us learn to talk.

We are a happy family. At least we were until about six months ago. Then the publishing company where my father has always worked moved to a new town, one hundred miles away.

My father is the editor of a magazine about farming. Nobody in the family wanted to move. But my father loves his job so, of course, he wanted to go with his company.

We bought a new house with a big yard that everybody liked, but it took a long time to get used to our new town. Before, my mom had always done all the shopping and banking for our family. Now she felt a little strange going into a store or bank where the clerks didn't know her. Very often she wanted Gina or me to go with her.

In our old town, everybody knew our family. Nobody stared when they saw us talking with our hands. But in the new town, people did stare. Of course, they pretended they didn't see us, but I knew they were looking.

It was even worse when my mom and dad talked. It seemed as if everyone looked at us when they heard my parents' strange-sounding voices. Sometimes Gina and I felt embarrassed, especially when we had to tell someone what my mother or father had said.

Gina and I didn't want to feel that way. We knew how shy our parents felt. We knew mom missed her art classes. We knew they both missed their old friends. We knew they were as lonesome and homesick as we were!

One awful day I saw three kids making fun of my parents. They were standing behind Mom and Dad and pretending to talk with their hands. I was so upset I wanted to pretend something, too. Just for a minute, I wanted to pretend my mother and father were not my parents. I had never felt that way before.

I was really so ashamed of myself.

That very same day Gina's favorite teacher gave her a note to take home. It was an invitation for our family to go to a performance of the National Theatre of the Deaf.

At first, I didn't want to give the invitation to my parents. I didn't want them to go. I didn't want people to make fun of them or feel sorry for Gina and me.

But Gina said they should go. She said that the play would be in sign language, and who would understand it better than our parents? I knew she was right. Besides, Mom and Dad needed to go out and meet new people.

Still, I was worried about what might happen. The night of the play, all sorts of questions were popping into my mind as I dragged up the steps into the hall. Then I saw those same three kids standing in the doorway. One of them grinned and wiggled his hands at me. That made me angry!

The big hall was filled with people. Just inside the door, my mother signed to me, "Where will we sit?"

To our surprise, a man stood up and said, "There are five seats over here."

We couldn't believe it. He was talking in sign language!

All around us, people were laughing and talking. Many of them were talking with their hands. They didn't seem to care who was watching.

Before the play started, we learned from our program that some of the actors were deaf and some could hear. The hearing actors and some of the deaf actors would speak in the play. All of the actors would sign, sometimes for themselves and sometimes for each other. Sometimes they would all sign together. Everyone in the audience would be able to understand what was going on.

The play we saw was called *The Wooden Boy*. It was about Pinocchio, a puppet who wanted to be a real boy. It was both funny and sad.

After the play, we went backstage to meet the actors. The deaf performers talked with people who knew sign language. The hearing performers helped the other people understand what was being said.

I was proud of my parents. They were smiling, and their fingers were flying as fast as anyone's. For the first time in many months, they seemed to feel at home.

Then we had another surprise. Gina's teacher came over to us. She talked very slowly and carefully so my mother could read her lips. Then she signed with her hands!

Gina was excited. Her favorite teacher, who wasn't deaf, had words in her hands, too. Gina was learning something she didn't know before. We all were. We were learning there were many friendly people in our new town who could talk with our parents. I decided this place wasn't going to be so bad, after all.

I think some hearing people around us were learning something, too—even those three kids, who were still following us around.

Maybe they never thought about it before, but being deaf doesn't mean you can't hear or talk. You can hear with your eyes and talk with your hands.

I'm glad that Gina and Diane and I know so many signs already. Why don't you learn a few yourself?

◆ LIBRARY LINK ◆

An interesting book about sign language is A Show of Hands *by Mary Beth Sullivan and Linda Bourke.*

Reader's Response

Who might have the hardest time getting used to the new town—Michael or his parents? Tell why.

Words In Our Hands

Thinking It Over

1. What were the different ways in which Michael's parents talked?
2. How did Michael's parents "hear" with their eyes?
3. Why did people in the new town stare at the family?
4. How did seeing *The Wooden Boy* make Michael feel? How do you know?
5. Why did Michael feel better about his family after seeing *The Wooden Boy*?

Writing to Learn

THINK AND DECIDE Do people "listen" with their eyes when they "talk" with their hands? Practice listening with your eyes. Tell what the children are saying with their gestures.

WRITE What did you learn about deafness? Tell one thing you will remember if you speak with a person who is hearing impaired.

275

Magazine

News About Reading

Words and Other Codes

This person is reading a mirror-code message.

You want to tell your friend a secret. No one else must know what you're saying. So the way to do it is to use a code that only the two of you will understand.

MEE TME AFT ERS CHO OL

See if you can figure out this secret message. It is a simple "space code." Words are broken up by spacing after every third letter. Here is what the code means:

MEET ME AFTER SCHOOL

Now try to figure this one out. You can figure it out by holding it up to a mirror.

CAN YOU COME TO MY

HOUSE ON SATURDAY?

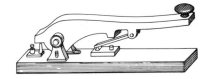

Samuel Morse made it possible to send messages over long distances instantly with his invention, the telegraph.

Not all codes are written. In the 1830s, Samuel Morse invented a new way to send messages by wire. His code uses dots and dashes to make letters and numbers. Dot-dot-dot means "S." Dash-dash-dash means "O." Dot-dot-dot again means "S." SOS means that a ship is in trouble.

What do codes have to do with reading? When you were first learning to read, all words looked like a code to you. By now you have come a long way in breaking the reading code, a process that is sometimes called decoding. You will continue to read words that are new to you. If you think of them as codes to break, figuring out new words can be fun.

S ●●●   O ▬▬▬   S ●●●

In Morse code, dots and dashes stand for letters and numbers.

☛ *If you want to learn more about writing and talking in code, read the book* How to Keep a Secret *by Elizabeth James and Carol Barkin. You can get ideas for codes from magazines, too. See the "Adventures of the Puzzle Squad" in* U.S. Kids *and "Pencil Power" in* Kid City.

277

In sports, messages to players often need to be kept secret from the other team. That's when sports signals become codes, and scratching an arm can mean something more than having an itch.

SPORTS SIGNALS

by Gary Apple

Imagine that you are the coach of a football team. Your team is behind by one point, and there is time for only one more play. The other team expects you to throw a long pass, but you decide to surprise them and run with the ball.

How do you communicate your plan to your players? You can't shout, "Surprise them by running instead of passing!" Your players may not hear you, and if they do, the other team will hear you, too. The surprise will be lost.

278

Can you tell which of these coaches is giving a signal?

Instead, you communicate by giving your team a
secret signal using sign language. Before the game, you
tell your team that if you put both hands on your head,
it means to run with the ball. Your players read your
signal and try to run with the ball. Success! Your team
scores, and you win the game!

Sign language is used all the time in sports.
Coaches signal players. Players signal other players.
Officials signal players, and players signal officials.
Everyone signals everybody!

Of course, signals aren't used only for secret plays. In football, for example, before a player catches a punt, he can wave his hand to signal a *fair catch*. With this signal the player makes a deal with the other team. It means, "If you don't try to tackle me, I won't try to run with the ball when I catch it."

Another sports signal that everyone understands and uses is the "time-out" sign. This is done by making a letter "T" with the hands. It tells the official to stop the clock. Football and basketball are two of the sports that use this sign.

Fair Catch!   **Time Out!**   **Safe!**

How many secret signals can you find in this picture?

Secret signals are used when one team doesn't want the other team to know what's going on. If you have ever watched a football game, you may have noticed a coach on the sidelines making strange movements. What he is doing is giving secret directions to the players on the field.

Football coaches can be very tricky. Sometimes, two coaches on the same team give signals at the same time. One coach gives the real secret play while the other gives signals that the players ignore. This is done to confuse the other team, so they don't know which signal is the real signal.

Baseball is the sport in which secret signals are used the most. When you watch a baseball game, it might look like the players are just waiting around for the next pitch. If you look closer, however, you will see that secret communications are being sent all over the field. If you see a player scratch his chin or a coach push his cap back on his head, there is a good chance that you have just seen a secret signal.

The catcher is about to signal for a certain type of pitch.

The pitcher and the catcher use sign language before every pitch. The catcher gives a sign to tell the pitcher the kind of pitch to throw. One finger may mean ''Throw a fastball.'' Two fingers may mean ''Pitch a curve ball.'' The catcher also uses a sign to tell the pitcher where to throw the pitch: inside, outside, high, or low. If the pitcher doesn't agree with the catcher, he will shake his head. The catcher will then secretly suggest another pitch.

Before every game, the catcher and the pitcher must talk about the sign language to be used. This way, there will be no mistakes. If a pitcher does not understand the signs, he might throw the wrong pitch, and the catcher may not be able to catch the ball.

The pitcher isn't the only one watching the catcher's secret signs. The second baseman and the shortstop also follow the sign language. If they know the kind of pitch to expect, they can guess where the ball will go if the batter hits it. The shortstop and second baseman have a set of secret signs of their own. They use them to tell the outfielders, who are far away and can't see the catcher, what kind of pitch is on the way. When a shortstop puts his hands on his knees, he might be telling the outfielders to expect a fastball.

The team that is up to bat also uses secret sign language. During a ballgame, coaches stand near first base and third base. Part of their job is to give secret directions to the batter. They also direct the runners who have reached a base. These coaches may seem to be just standing around, but don't be fooled. When they dust off their sleeve or hold their elbow, they may be telling the batter to bunt or the base runner to steal a base.

A base coach secretly signals batters and base runners.

283

Teams are always trying to find out what the other team's signals are. To stop this from happening, teams often change their signals during a game. A sign that meant "steal the base" in one inning may mean "stay on base" in another. Coaches can get even trickier than that. For example, base runners might be told to ignore all signs unless the coach's feet are in a certain position.

The next time you're at the ballpark or stadium, pay attention to the movements of the team members. See if you can tell which are secret signals and which are everyday movements. Players and coaches can be tricky, so watch carefully; but don't be too suspicious. When a coach scratches his chin, he might just have an itch!

◆ LIBRARY LINK ◆

If you would like to learn more about signals, you might enjoy reading Train Whistles *by Helen Roney Settler.*

Reader's Response

Do you think understanding sports signals will help you enjoy sports more? Why or why not?

SPORTS SIGNALS

Thinking It Over

1. Why are signals used in sports?
2. How are the signals for *fair catch* and *time out* different from the other signals described?
3. Who gives secret signals in baseball?
4. A team often changes its secret signals. Why is this helpful? How might it be a problem? How did you decide on your answers?
5. In which sports do you think secret signals would not be useful?

Writing to Learn

THINK AND CREATE   You, also, may create a secret language. If you want to send a message in code, put the first letter of each word at the end. Read the code chart below.

Real Word	Code Word
sports	portss
signal	ignals
message	essagem

WRITE   Write a message to a friend. Write it in code. See if your friend can figure out the message.

LITERATURE LINK

How can you make predictions when you read?

Charlie Brown guessed that Snoopy needed help. He soon found out that Snoopy can take care of himself!

When you read, do you guess what's going to happen next? That's called making predictions. Making predictions keeps you involved in the story. It keeps you thinking as you read. You may guess wrong, but that's not important. You can always change your mind. After all, who could have predicted what Snoopy would do?

What's Next?

When you read this part of the story "Forecast," did you predict what would happen next?

———◦◦———

Theodore yeowled with laughter. "Snow? Did you say *snow*? Caroline, look outside. It's the middle of summer!"

Caroline folded her arms stubbornly across her chest. "My instruments say it will snow on Friday. Anyway, every now and then it does snow in the summer. In July of 1816, for example…"

———◦◦———

Theodore thought Caroline was wrong! Did you? What helped you decide? Did you change your mind as you read more of the story?

The tips below will help you make predictions when you read.

- Think about what is happening. Is it like anything you know about?
- Guess what might happen next.
- Read to find out if you are right.
- As you get more information, change your prediction if you need to.
- Keep thinking as you go.

As you read "The Horse Who Lived Upstairs," try to guess what will happen next. Use the tips above to stay involved in the story.

The Horse Who Lived Upstairs

by Phyllis McGinley

Joey was a city horse who wanted to live in the country. Then one day, Joey got his wish!

There was once a horse named Joey who was discontented. He was discontented because he didn't live in a red barn with a weathervane on top like this, and he didn't live in a green meadow where he could run about and kick up his heels like this. Instead, he lived upstairs in a big brick building in New York.

Joey worked for Mr. Polaski, who sold fruits and vegetables to city people. Joey pulled the vegetable wagon through the city streets. And in New York, there isn't room for barns or meadows.

So every night when Joey came home, he stepped out from the shafts of the wagon and into an elevator, and up he went to his stall on the fourth floor of the big brick building. It was a fine stall and Joey was very comfortable there. He had plenty of oats to eat and plenty of fresh straw to lie on. He even had a window to look out of. But still Joey was discontented.

"How I long to sip fresh water from a babbling brook!" he often exclaimed. And then he would sniff discontentedly at the old bathtub near the elevator that served him as a watering trough.

It wasn't that he had to work hard. Mr. Polaski was kind to him and brought him home at five o'clock every day.

In the winter Joey had a blanket to wear on his back to keep him warm. And in the summertime Mr. Polaski got him a hat to wear on his head to keep him cool. And every day he had many interesting adventures. Sometimes he met a policeman who gave him sugar. Sometimes ladies patted him on the nose and fed him carrots. He was introduced to the high-bred horses who drew the hansom cabs along the plaza. He saw the children playing in the playgrounds and the parks. But it made no difference to Joey.

"This is no life for a horse," he used to say to the Percheron who lived in the next stall to him. "We city horses don't know what real living is. I want to move to the country and sleep in a red barn with a weathervane on top and kick up my heels in a green meadow."

So how happy he was when one day Mr. Polaski said to him, "Joey, I think I could sell more vegetables if I drove a truck. I will miss you, Joey, but you will like it on the farm where I am going to send you."

When Joey reached the country, sure enough, there was the barn with its weathervane, and there was the meadow.

"This is the life!" cried Joey to himself. But poor Joey! The barn was cold in winter and hot in summer. He didn't have a blanket and he didn't have a hat. And he had very little time to kick up his heels in the green meadow, for all day long he pulled a plow through the earth. A plow is harder to pull than a wagon, and besides, the farmer worked from sunrise to sundown instead of the eight hours Joey was used to. Sometimes they forgot to put fresh straw in his stall, and nobody thought to give him sugar or carrots. There were plenty of children but they climbed on his back and teased him when he wanted to eat. And instead of the Percheron, there was a cross old gray horse next to him, who looked down his nose at Joey because Joey knew so little about farm life.

One day, when he wasn't pulling a plow because it was Sunday, Joey saw several people picnicking in the meadow. He decided to join them, for they looked as if they came from the city, and he thought they might have a lump of sugar in one of their pockets.

When he reached the spot, they had gone for a walk, so he ate up their lunch. When they came back, they were very angry and Joey was shut up in his stall for the rest of the day. He didn't even have a window to look out of. He was lonely for his friends, the policeman and the ladies who patted him on the nose. He was lonely for the high-bred horses and all the interesting sights of the city.

"I don't think I belong in the country after all," sighed Joey. "I am now more discontented than ever."

Next day he heard the honk of a horn. He looked from the door of the barn, and whom should he see but Mr. Polaski, getting out of the truck!

"I have come for Joey," Mr. Polaski told the farmer. "I cannot get any more tires for my truck, so I think I will sell fruit and vegetables from my wagon again."

My goodness, but Joey was happy! He went back to the city with Mr. Polaski and got into the elevator, and up he went to the fourth floor of the big brick building. There was his stall, and there was the window for him to look out of. And there was the friendly Percheron.

"Welcome back, Joey," exclaimed the Percheron. "I have missed you. The policeman has missed you. The lady customers have missed you, and so have the children in the playgrounds and the parks. Tell me, how did you like the country?"

"The country is all right for country animals," Joey said, "but I guess I am just a city horse at heart."

And he was never discontented again.

 Reader's Response

What surprised you in this story?

The Horse Who Lived
Upstairs

Thinking It Over

1. What did Joey wish for?
2. How did people show that they cared about Joey? Tell how you got your answer.
3. Compare Joey's life in the city with his life on the farm.
4. What made Joey finally realize that he belonged in the city?
5. Do you think Mr. Polaski took Joey back because he really couldn't get tires for his truck? Explain.

Writing to Learn

THINK AND ANALYZE How did Joey feel about the country before he went there? How did he feel about it after he got there? Copy and finish the chart below.

How Joey Felt About the Country...	
Before He Went There	After He Went There
The country was nice.	

WRITE Read what you wrote in the chart. Then write a sentence to tell how you think Joey might have felt when Mr. Polaski said, "I have come for Joey."

A young woman expresses kindness to everyone she meets. Even the king learns of her goodness— in a most surprising way.

MUFARO'S *Beautiful* DAUGHTERS

AN AFRICAN TALE

written and illustrated by John Steptoe

A long time ago, in a certain place in Africa,
a small village lay across a river and half a day's
journey from a city where a great king lived. A man
named Mufaro (əm fä' rō) lived in this village with his
two daughters, who were called Manyara (män yä' rə)
and Nyasha (nyä' shə). Everyone agreed that Manyara
and Nyasha were very beautiful.

Manyara was almost always in a bad temper. She teased her sister whenever their father's back was turned, and she had been heard to say, "Someday, Nyasha, I will be a queen, and you will be a servant in my household."

"If that should come to pass," Nyasha responded, "I will be pleased to serve you. But why do you say such things? You are clever and strong and beautiful. Why are you so unhappy?"

"Because everyone talks about how kind *you* are, and they praise everything you do," Manyara replied. "I'm certain that Father loves you best. But when I am a queen, everyone will know that your silly kindness is only weakness."

Nyasha was sad that Manyara felt this way, but she ignored her sister's words and went about her chores. Nyasha kept a small plot of land, on which she grew millet, sunflowers, yams, and vegetables. She always sang as she worked, and some said it was her singing that made her crops more bountiful than anyone else's.

One day, Nyasha noticed a small garden snake resting beneath a yam vine. "Good day, little Nyoka (nyō' kä)," she called to him. "You are welcome here. You will keep away any creatures who might spoil my vegetables." She bent forward, gave the little snake a loving pat on the head, and then returned to her work.

From that day on, Nyoka was always at Nyasha's side when she tended her garden. It was said that she sang all the more sweetly when he was there.

Mufaro knew nothing of how Manyara treated Nyasha. Nyasha was too considerate of her father's feelings to complain, and Manyara was always careful to behave herself when Mufaro was around.

Early one morning, a messenger from the city arrived. The Great King wanted a wife. "The Most Worthy and Beautiful Daughters in the Land are invited to appear before the King, and he will choose one to become Queen!" the messenger proclaimed.

Mufaro called Manyara and Nyasha to him. "It would be a great honor to have one of you chosen," he said. "Prepare yourselves to journey to the city. I will call together all our friends to make a wedding party. We will leave tomorrow as the sun rises."

"But, my father," Manyara said sweetly, "it would be painful for either of us to leave you, even to be wife to the king. I know Nyasha would grieve to death if she were parted from you. I am strong. Send me to the city, and let poor Nyasha be happy here with you."

Mufaro beamed with pride. "The king has asked for the most worthy and the most beautiful. No, Manyara, I cannot send you alone. Only a king can choose between two such worthy daughters. Both of you must go!"

That night, when everyone was asleep, Manyara stole quietly out of the village. She had never been in the forest at night before, and she was frightened, but her greed to be the first to appear before the king drove her on. In her hurry, she almost stumbled over a small boy who suddenly appeared, standing in the path.

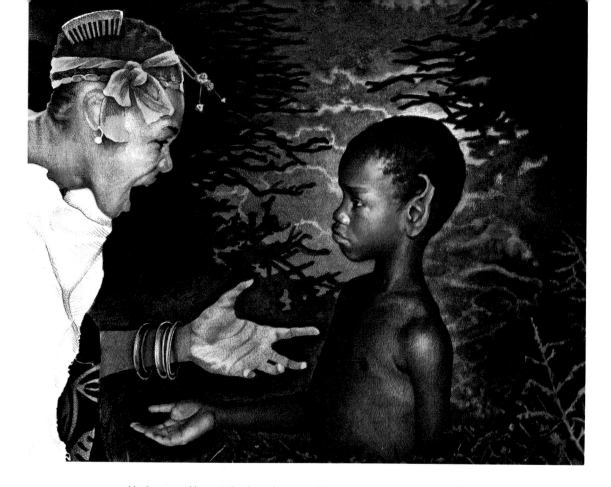

"Please," said the boy. "I am hungry. Will you
give me something to eat?"

"I have brought only enough for myself,"
Manyara replied.

"But, please!" said the boy. "I am so *very*
hungry."

"Out of my way, boy! Tomorrow I will become
your queen. How dare you stand in my path?"

After traveling for what seemed to be a great
distance, Manyara came to a small clearing. There,
silhouetted against the moonlight, was an old woman
seated on a large stone.

The old woman spoke. "I will give you some advice, Manyara. Soon after you pass the place where two paths cross, you will see a grove of trees. They will laugh at you. You must not laugh in return. Later, you will meet a man with his head under his arm. You must be polite to him."

"How do you know my name? How dare you advise your future queen? Stand aside, you ugly old woman!" Manyara scolded, and then rushed on her way without looking back.

Just as the old woman had foretold, Manyara came to a grove of trees, and they did indeed seem to be laughing at her.

"I must be calm," Manyara thought. "I will *not* be frightened." She looked up at the trees and laughed out loud. "I laugh at you, trees!" she shouted, and she hurried on.

It was not yet dawn when Manyara heard the sound of rushing water. "The river must be up ahead," she thought. "The great city is just on the other side."

But there, on the rise, she saw a man with his head tucked under his arm. Manyara ran past him without speaking. "A queen acknowledges only those who please her," she said to herself. "I will be queen. I will be queen," she chanted, as she hurried on toward the city.

Nyasha woke at the first light of dawn. As she put on her finest garments, she thought how her life might be changed forever beyond this day. "I'd much prefer to live here," she admitted to herself. "I'd hate to leave this village and never see my father or sing to little Nyoka again."

Her thoughts were interrupted by loud shouts and a commotion from the wedding party assembled outside. Manyara was missing! Everyone bustled about, searching and calling for her. When they found her footprints on the path that led to the city, they decided to go on as planned.

As the wedding party moved through the forest, brightly plumed birds darted about in the cool green shadows beneath the trees. Though anxious about her sister, Nyasha was soon filled with excitement about all there was to see.

They were deep in the forest when she saw the small boy standing by the side of the path.

"You must be hungry," she said, and handed him a yam she had brought for her lunch. The boy smiled and disappeared as quietly as he had come.

Later, as they were approaching the place where the two paths crossed, the old woman appeared and silently pointed the way to the city. Nyasha thanked her and gave her a small pouch filled with sunflower seeds.

The sun was high in the sky when the party came to the grove of towering trees. Their uppermost branches seemed to bow down to Nyasha as she passed beneath them.

At last, someone announced that they were near their destination.

Nyasha ran ahead and topped the rise before the others could catch up with her. She stood transfixed at her first sight of the city. "Oh, my father," she called. "A great spirit must stand guard here! Just look at what lies before us. I never in all my life dreamed there could be anything so beautiful!"

Arm in arm, Nyasha and her father descended the hill, crossed the river, and approached the city gate. Just as they entered through the great doors, the air was rent by piercing cries, and Manyara ran wildly out of a chamber at the center of the enclosure. When she saw Nyasha, she fell upon her, sobbing.

"Do not go to the king, my sister. Oh, please, Father, do not let her go!" she cried hysterically. "There's a great monster there, a snake with five heads! He said that he knew all my faults and that I displeased him. He would have swallowed me alive if I had not run. Oh, my sister, please do not go inside that place."

It frightened Nyasha to see her sister so upset. But, leaving her father to comfort Manyara, she bravely made her way to the chamber and opened the door.

On the seat of the great chief's stool lay the little garden snake. Nyasha laughed with relief and joy.

"My little friend," she exclaimed. "It's such a pleasure to see you, but why are you here?"

"I am the king," Nyoka replied.

And there, before Nyasha's eyes, the garden snake changed shape.

"I am the king. I am also the hungry boy with whom you shared a yam in the forest and the old woman to whom you made a gift of sunflower seeds. But you know me best as Nyoka. Because I have been all of these, I know you to be the Most Worthy and Most Beautiful Daughter in the Land. It would make me very happy if you would be my wife."

And so it was that, a long time ago, Nyasha agreed to be married. The king's mother and sisters took Nyasha to their house, and the wedding preparations began. The best weavers in the land laid out their finest cloth for her wedding garments. Villagers from all around were invited to the celebration, and a great feast was held. Nyasha prepared the bread for the wedding feast from millet that had been brought from her village.

Mufaro declared to all who would hear him that he was the happiest father in all the land, for he was blessed with two beautiful and worthy daughters— Nyasha, the queen; and Manyara, a servant in the queen's household.

◆ LIBRARY LINK ◆

If you enjoyed reading this story by John Steptoe, you might like to read other books by this author, such as Train Ride.

Reader's Response

What pictures does this story create in your mind?

MUFARO'S BEAUTIFUL DAUGHTERS

Thinking It Over

1. How did Manyara feel toward her sister?
2. What was the real reason Manyara told her father that Nyasha should not leave home?
3. Why did the king appear to the sisters in so many different forms?
4. How did the king test Manyara and Nyasha? Tell some of the ways.
5. Do you think Manyara's behavior changed after what happened to her? How did you reach this conclusion?

Writing to Learn

THINK AND INVENT   Many characters are in this story: Mufaro, Manyara, Nyasha, and the king who takes many shapes and forms. Read the character riddle below.

Character Riddle

I am a little creature.
I stay by Nyasha's side.
I like to hear her sing.
Who am I?

(Nyoka the snake)

WRITE   Write a character riddle about one of the characters in the story. You may tell what the character says or does. See if others can guess your riddle.

LITERATURE LINK

Why are plays fun to read?

Picture yourself on a stage. You're in a costume. In front of you is an audience. You're in a play!

Looking Closely at a Play

A play is a story for people to act out. Sometimes, a writer will rewrite a story as a play. This lets the readers take part in the action. They can talk and act like the characters.

Here is a small part of the play "The Musicians of Bremen Town." You may have read the fairy tale as a story. Notice how the play looks different from the story.

NARRATOR: Now they were a very sad donkey, and cat, and dog, and rooster. *(All moan and cry.)* They didn't know what they could do. *(All shake their heads.)* They had to leave the farm. *(All nod.)* But where could they go, and what could they do to earn a living? *(All shrug.)* Then the donkey had an idea.

DONKEY: I have an idea!

CAT, DOG, *and* ROOSTER *(Excitedly)*: What? What?

DONKEY: Why don't we become famous singers? *(All look at him in surprise.)*

Here are some things you may have noticed. This play has a narrator who tells part of the story. The name of each character tells who is speaking. Often the speaking parts include directions that tell the characters what to do.

The following story, "The Boy Who Cried Wolf," is a famous fable rewritten as a play. Notice that the play is divided into acts. One of the acts is divided into scenes. Scenes let you know when there is a change in time or place.

In this play, a young shepherd boy learns a lesson . . . and so do we.

The Boy Who Cried WOLF

from the fable by Aesop
adapted by Genie Iverson

Characters: Storyteller   Little Girl
Shepherd Boy   First Farmhand
Father   Second Farmhand
Old Woman   Third Farmhand
Farmer

ACT ONE

Storyteller: A shepherd boy and his father stand talking on a hillside. Their sheep move about them.

Father: Are you ready to look after these sheep by yourself, son? It's time for me to go back to the village.

Shepherd Boy: (*uncertain*) I think so, Papa.

Father: I'll help you herd our sheep here each morning. And I'll come back at sunset to help you drive them home. But you must stay with them during the day.

Shepherd Boy: Yes, Papa. Only . . . (*looking around*) . . . I don't think I'll like being up here alone.

Father: Alone? Nonsense! Look down there at the road. People come and go all day.

Shepherd Boy: But they never stop.

Father: Maybe they don't stop. But they will come if you ever need help. Just call. (*handing boy the crook*) I have to go now. But I'll be back at sunset. (Father *leaves and the shepherd sits down to watch his sheep.*)

Storyteller: Slowly—very slowly the morning passes. The young shepherd boy feels more and more alone.

Shepherd Boy: I don't like staying here all day by myself. (*sighs*) It's lonely here.

Storyteller: Looking down the hill, the shepherd boy sees an old woman walking along the road. Pails of milk swing from a pole across her shoulders.

Shepherd Boy: I wish that old woman would stop and visit. I wish . . . (*pause*) . . . I know what I'll do! (*leaps up waving his crook*) Help! Help! A WOLF is after my sheep!

Storyteller: The old woman hurries up the hill to help. Milk splashes from her pails.

Old Woman: (*winded*) Where? . . . Where is the wolf? We can chase him with my pole!

Shepherd Boy: (*looking down*) There is no wolf. I wanted you to stop and visit. So I played a trick on you.

Old Woman: No wolf! You mean you made me run up this hill for nothing? What is the matter with you, boy?

Shepherd Boy: I didn't mean any harm.

Old Woman: (*picking up her pails*) Hummf! Just look at these pails! Empty! All that good milk . . . spilled for nothing.

Shepherd Boy: I just wanted you to stop and visit. . . .

Old Woman: Tricking folks is a sorry business. I came to visit you today, but trouble may be your visitor tomorrow. Mark my words. (*walking away muttering*) He'll be sorry . . . sorry indeed. Just wait and see!

ACT TWO

Storyteller: It is the next morning. The unhappy shepherd boy sits on the hillside. As his sheep move about him, he thinks about the long, lonely day ahead.

Shepherd Boy: (*wearily*) Nibble . . . Nibble . . . Nibble!

Baaaa! . . . Baaaa! . . . Baaaa!

Nibble . . . Baaaa!

Baaaa! . . . Nibble! (*long sigh*)

All day long . . . that's all you old sheep ever do!

Storyteller: The shepherd boy hears the rumble of a cart.

Shepherd Boy: Listen! Someone's coming! (*stands and looks down the hill*)

Storyteller: A farmer and his little girl appear on the road, pulling a cart filled with turnips.

Shepherd Boy: Do I dare call out again that there is a wolf? If I do . . . maybe they'll stop. . . . (*pause*) . . . Help! Help! A wolf is after my sheep!

Storyteller: The farmer leaves his cart and runs up the hill to help. His little girl hurries along behind.

Farmer: Where? Where's the wolf?

Little Girl: (*afraid*) Is the wolf hiding behind that tree? Will he eat me?

Farmer: I don't see any wolf. (*looking around*) There's no wolf here!

Shepherd Boy: It was just a trick.

Farmer: (*angrily*) You called for help when you didn't need it! Shame on you!

Shepherd Boy: Please don't be angry. I get lonely sitting here all day by myself.

Farmer: (*taking* little girl *by hand*) Come along, child. This boy has wasted enough of our time with his tricks. But someday he'll be sorry.

Little Girl: (*as they walk away*) Why will he be sorry, Papa?

Farmer: Because tricks bring trouble. Just wait and see. What that boy did today will be remembered tomorrow. (*They exit.*)

ACT THREE
(Scene One)

Storyteller: It is another bright, cool morning. The shepherd boy has watched his flock since sunrise. He is bored and lonely.

Shepherd Boy: Same old hillside! (*sigh*) Same old sheep! Same old grass! And the sun is not even overhead yet. It's still morning! (*long sigh*) Maybe I'll sit and watch the road. Somebody should be coming along soon.

Storyteller: The shepherd boy is about to sit when he hears a loud growl. He turns. A wolf is crouched near his flock.

Shepherd Boy: A WOLF! (*He crawls behind a rock and peeks out.*) A REAL wolf! What can I do!

Storyteller: As the wolf creeps nearer to the frightened sheep, singing is heard from the road below.

Farmhands: (*offstage*) Hey, ho! Hey, ho!
It's to the fields we go,
With hoe and rake,
With rake and hoe,
Hey, ho! Hey, ho!

Storyteller: Three farmhands come into view. The shepherd boy runs to the top of the hill shouting.

Shepherd Boy: (*waving his crook*) HELP! HELP! A WOLF is after my sheep!

First Farmhand: (*stopping*) Look. It's that shepherd boy! The one folks are talking about.

Second Farmhand: They say he cries "wolf" when there is no wolf.

Third Farmhand: (*nodding*) Foolish boy! You can't believe a word he says.

Shepherd Boy: (*calling as loudly as he can*) Hurry! Hurry! The wolf is taking my sheep!

First Farmhand: (*calling to shepherd*) We DON'T believe you!

Second Farmhand: That's right! We've heard about you and your tricks.

Third Farmhand: You can't fool us! We know there is no wolf! (*The farmhands walk away laughing.*)

Shepherd Boy: Come back! Come back! This ISN'T a trick. This time there IS a wolf! A REAL wolf! . . . (*sobs*) . . . He is running away with my sheep. (*The boy sits down, covers his face with his hands and cries.*)

(Scene Two)

Storyteller: It is sunset. The shepherd sits with his head in his hands. The wolf is gone. But so are some of the sheep. Father approaches.

Father: Are you ready to take the sheep home?

Shepherd Boy: Oh yes, Papa! But some of the sheep are gone! A wolf came—a great big wolf!

Father: A wolf! Did you call for help?

Shepherd Boy: Yes, Papa. Yes. There were men on the road. I called. But they wouldn't come. (*lowering his eyes*) They thought that I was playing a trick.

Father: (*puzzled*) A trick?

Shepherd Boy: (*hanging his head*) Before when I was lonely, I cried "wolf" so that people would stop and visit. Then . . . then there really was a wolf. And I called. But they didn't believe me.

Father: (*sitting down on a rock*) Well . . . have you learned something?

Shepherd Boy: (*sitting down beside his father*) Yes, Papa. I learned that I should always tell the truth . . . (*pause*) . . . because if I don't, people won't believe me when I do.

THE END

◆ LIBRARY LINK ◆

If you enjoyed this play based on a tale by Aesop, you might want to read Aesop's Fables, *edited by Anne White, or* Tales from Aesop, *edited by Harold Jones.*

Reader's Response

How did you feel about the lesson in this play?

The Boy Who Cried
WOLF

Thinking It Over

1. Why did the boy call for help the first two times?
2. What did the farmer mean when he said that what the boy did today would be remembered tomorrow?
3. Was the farmer correct? Tell why or why not.
4. Why do you think that the boy's father didn't punish him?
5. What words would you use to describe the boy in this story? Why did you choose these words?

Writing to Learn

THINK AND IMAGINE The young shepherd boy learns many things about himself and his friends. Imagine what he might have written in his journal.

> One day, a real wolf came and

WRITE Pretend you are the shepherd boy. On a page of your notebook, write about your frightening day. Tell how your adventure may have changed your life forever.

323

Sometimes, as friends talk, the message gets all mixed up. This certainly is true for Piglet and Pooh.

In Which Piglet Meets a Heffalump

from
Winnie-the-Pooh

written by A. A. Milne
illustrated by Ernest H. Shepard

*Piglet and Winnie-the-Pooh are two of
Christopher Robin's stuffed animals. He brings them
to life in his imagination, where they have many
interesting and funny adventures.*

One day, when Christopher Robin and Winnie-the-Pooh and Piglet were all talking together, Christopher Robin finished the mouthful he was eating and said carelessly: "I saw a Heffalump to-day, Piglet."

"What was it doing?" asked Piglet.

"Just lumping along," said Christopher Robin. "I don't think it saw *me*."

"I saw one once," said Piglet. "At least, I think I did," he said. "Only perhaps it wasn't."

"So did I," said Pooh, wondering what a Heffalump was like.

"You don't often see them," said Christopher Robin carelessly.

"Not now," said Piglet.

"Not at this time of year," said Pooh.

Then they all talked about something else, until it was time for Pooh and Piglet to go home together.

At first as they stumped along the path which edged the Hundred Acre Wood, they didn't say much to each other; but when they came to the stream and had helped each other across the stepping stones, and were able to walk side by side again over the heather, they began to talk in a friendly way about this and that, and Piglet said, "If you see what I mean, Pooh," and Pooh said, "It's just what I think myself, Piglet," and Piglet said, "But, on the other hand, Pooh, we must remember," and Pooh said, "Quite true, Piglet, although I had forgotten it for the moment." And then, just as they came to the Six Pine Trees, Pooh looked round to see that nobody else was listening, and said in a very solemn voice:

"Piglet, I have decided something."

"What have you decided, Pooh?"

"I have decided to catch a Heffalump."

Pooh nodded his head several times as he said this, and waited for Piglet to say "How?" or "Pooh, you couldn't!" or something helpful of that sort, but Piglet said nothing. The fact was Piglet was wishing that *he* had thought about it first.

"I shall do it," said Pooh, after waiting a little longer, "by means of a trap. And it must be a Cunning Trap, so you will have to help me, Piglet."

"Pooh," said Piglet, feeling quite happy again now, "I will." And then he said, "How shall we do it?" and Pooh said, "That's just it. How?" And then they sat down together to think it out.

Pooh's first idea was that they should dig a Very Deep Pit, and then the Heffalump would come along and fall into the Pit, and——

"Why?" said Piglet.

"Why what?" said Pooh.

"Why would he fall in?"

Pooh rubbed his nose with his paw, and said that the Heffalump might be walking along, humming a little song, and looking up at the sky, wondering if it would rain, and so he wouldn't see the Very Deep Pit until he was half-way down, when it would be too late.

Piglet said that this was a very good Trap, but supposing it were raining already?

Pooh rubbed his nose again, and said that he hadn't thought of that. And then he brightened up, and said that, if it were raining already, the Heffalump

would be looking at the sky wondering if it would *clear up,* and so he wouldn't see the Very Deep Pit until he was half-way down. . . . When it would be too late.

Piglet said that, now that this point had been explained, he thought it was a Cunning Trap.

Pooh was very proud when he heard this, and he felt that the Heffalump was as good as caught already, but there was just one other thing which had to be thought about, and it was this. *Where should they dig the Very Deep Pit?*

Piglet said that the best place would be somewhere where a Heffalump was, just before he fell into it, only about a foot farther on.

"But then he would see us digging it," said Pooh.

"Not if he was looking at the sky."

"He would Suspect," said Pooh, "if he happened to look down." He thought for a long time and then added sadly, "It isn't as easy as I thought. I suppose that's why Heffalumps hardly *ever* get caught."

"That must be it," said Piglet.

They sighed and got up; and when they had taken a few gorse prickles out of themselves they sat down again; and all the time Pooh was saying to himself, "If only I could *think* of something!" For he felt sure that a Very Clever Brain could catch a Heffalump if only he knew the right way to go about it.

"Suppose," he said to Piglet, "*you* wanted to catch *me*, how would you do it?"

"Well," said Piglet, "I should do it like this. I should make a Trap, and I should put a Jar of Honey in the Trap, and you would smell it, and you would go in after it, and——"

"And I would go in after it," said Pooh excitedly, "only very carefully so as not to hurt myself, and I would get to the Jar of Honey, and I should lick round the edges first of all, pretending that there wasn't any more, you know, and then I should walk away and think about it a little, and then I should come back and start licking in the middle of the jar, and then——"

"Yes, well never mind about that. There you would be, and there I should catch you. Now the first thing to think of is, What do Heffalumps like? I should think acorns, shouldn't you? We'll get a lot of—I say, wake up, Pooh!"

Pooh, who had gone into a happy dream, woke up with a start, and said that Honey was a much more trappy thing than Haycorns. Piglet didn't think so; and they were just going to argue about it, when Piglet remembered that, if they put acorns in the Trap, *he* would have to find the acorns, but if they put honey, then Pooh would have to give up some of his own honey, so he said, "All right, honey then," just as Pooh remembered it too, and was going to say, "All right, haycorns."

"Honey," said Piglet to himself in a thoughtful way, as if it were now settled. "*I'll* dig the pit, while *you* go and get the honey."

"Very well," said Pooh, and he stumped off.

As soon as he got home, he went to the larder; and he stood on a chair, and took down a very large jar of honey from the top shelf. It had HUNNY written on it, but, just to make sure, he took off the paper cover and looked at it, and it *looked* just like honey. "But you never can tell," said Pooh. "I remember my uncle saying once that he had seen cheese just this colour." So he put his tongue in, and took a large lick. "Yes," he said, "it is. No doubt about that. And honey, I should say, right down to the bottom of the jar. Unless, of course," he said, "somebody put cheese in at the bottom just for a joke. Perhaps I had better go a *little* further . . . just in case . . . in case Heffalumps *don't* like cheese . . . same as me. . . . Ah!" And he gave a deep sigh. "I *was* right. It *is* honey, right the way down."

Having made certain of this, he took the jar back to Piglet, and Piglet looked up from the bottom of his Very Deep Pit, and said, "Got it?" and Pooh said, "Yes, but it isn't quite a full jar," and he threw it down to Piglet, and Piglet said, "No, it isn't! Is that all you've got left?" and Pooh said "Yes." Because it was. So Piglet put the jar at the bottom of the Pit, and climbed out, and they went off home together.

"Well, good night, Pooh," said Piglet, when they had got to Pooh's house. "And we meet at six o'clock tomorrow morning by the Pine Trees, and see how many Heffalumps we've got in our Trap."

"Six o'clock, Piglet. And have you got any string?"

"No. Why do you want string?"

"To lead them home with."

"Oh! . . . I *think* Heffalumps come if you whistle."

"Some do and some don't. You never can tell with Heffalumps. Well, good night!"

"Good night!"

And off Piglet trotted to his house TRESPASSERS W, while Pooh made his preparations for bed.

Some hours later, just as the night was beginning to steal away, Pooh woke up suddenly with a sinking feeling. He had had that sinking feeling before, and he knew what it meant. *He was hungry.* So he went to the larder, and he stood on a chair and reached up to the top shelf, and found—nothing.

"That's funny," he thought. "I know I had a jar of honey there. A full jar, full of honey right up to the top, and it had HUNNY written on it, so that I should know it was honey. That's very funny." And then he began to wander up and down, wondering where it was and murmuring a murmur to himself. Like this:

It's very, very funny,
'Cos I *know* I had some honey;
'Cos it had a label on,
   Saying HUNNY.

A goloptious full-up pot too,
And I don't know where it's got to,
No, I don't know where it's gone—
   Well, it's funny.

He had murmured this to himself three times in a singing sort of way, when suddenly he remembered. He had put it into the Cunning Trap to catch the Heffalump.

"Bother!" said Pooh. "It all comes of trying to be kind to Heffalumps." And he got back into bed.

But he couldn't sleep. The more he tried to sleep, the more he couldn't. He tried Counting Sheep, which is sometimes a good way of getting to sleep, and, as that was no good, he tried counting Heffalumps. And that was worse. Because every Heffalump that he counted was making straight for a pot of Pooh's honey, *and eating it all.* For some minutes he lay there miserably, but when the five hundred and eighty-seventh Heffalump was licking its jaws, and saying to itself, "Very good honey this, I don't know when I've tasted better," Pooh could bear it no longer. He jumped out of bed, he ran out of the house, and he ran straight to the Six Pine Trees.

The Sun was still in bed, but there was a lightness in the sky over the Hundred Acre Wood which seemed to show that it was waking up and would soon be kicking off the clothes. In the half-light the Pine Trees looked cold and lonely, and the Very Deep Pit seemed deeper than it was, and Pooh's jar of honey at the bottom was something mysterious, a shape and no more. But as he got nearer to it his nose told him that it was indeed honey, and his tongue came out and began to polish up his mouth, ready for it.

"Bother!" said Pooh, as he got his nose inside the jar. "A Heffalump has been eating it!" And then he thought a little and said, "Oh, no, *I* did. I forgot."

Indeed, he had eaten most of it. But there was a little left at the very bottom of the jar, and he pushed his head right in, and began to lick. . . .

By and by Piglet woke up. As soon as he woke he said to himself, "Oh!" Then he said bravely, "Yes," and then, still more bravely, "Quite so." But he didn't feel very brave, for the word which was really jiggeting about in his brain was "Heffalumps."

What was a Heffalump like?

Was it Fierce?

Did it come when you whistled? And *how* did it come?

Was it Fond of Pigs at all?

If it was Fond of Pigs, did it make any difference *what sort of Pig?*

Supposing it was Fierce with Pigs, would it make any difference *if the Pig had a grandfather called TRESPASSERS WILLIAM?*

He didn't know the answer to any of these questions . . . and he was going to see his first Heffalump in about an hour from now!

Of course Pooh would be with him, and it was much more Friendly with two. But suppose Heffalumps were Very Fierce with Pigs *and* Bears? Wouldn't it be better to pretend that he had a headache, and couldn't go up to the Six Pine Trees this morning? But then suppose that it was a very fine day, and there was no Heffalump in the trap, here he would be, in bed all the morning, simply wasting his time for nothing. What should he do?

And then he had a Clever Idea. He would go up very quietly to the Six Pine Trees now, peep very cautiously into the Trap, and see if there *was* a Heffalump there. And if there was, he would go back to bed, and if there wasn't, he wouldn't.

So off he went. At first he thought that there wouldn't be a Heffalump in the Trap, and then he thought that there would, and as he got nearer he was *sure* that there would, because he could hear it heffalumping about it like anything.

"Oh, dear, oh, dear, oh, dear!" said Piglet to himself. And he wanted to run away. But somehow, having got so near, he felt that he must just see what a Heffalump was like. So he crept to the side of the Trap and looked in. . . .

And all the time Winnie-the-Pooh had been trying to get the honey-jar off his head. The more he shook it, the more tightly it stuck. "*Bother!*" he said, inside the jar, and "*Oh, help!*" and, mostly "*Ow!*" And he tried bumping it against things, but as he couldn't see what he was bumping it against, it didn't help him; and he tried to climb out of the Trap, but as he could see nothing but jar, and not much of that, he couldn't find his way. So at last he lifted up his head, jar and all, and made a loud, roaring noise of Sadness and Despair . . . and it was at that moment that Piglet looked down.

"Help, help!" cried Piglet, "a Heffalump, a Horrible Heffalump!" and he scampered off as hard as he could, still crying out, "Help, help, a Herrible Hoffalump! Hoff, Hoff, a Hellible Horralump! Holl, Holl, a Hoffable Hellerump!" And he didn't stop crying and scampering until he got to Christopher Robin's house.

"Whatever's the matter, Piglet?" said Christopher Robin, who was just getting up.

"Heff," said Piglet, breathing so hard that he could hardly speak, "a Hell—a Heff—a Heffalump."

"Where?"

"Up there," said Piglet, waving his paw.

"What did it look like?"

"Like—like——It had the biggest head you ever saw, Christopher Robin. A great enormous thing, like—like nothing. A huge big—well, like a—I don't know—like an enormous big nothing. Like a jar."

"Well," said Christopher Robin, putting on his shoes, "I shall go and look at it. Come on."

Piglet wasn't afraid if he had Christopher Robin with him, so off they went. . . .

"I can hear it, can't you?" said Piglet anxiously, as they got near.

"I can hear *something*," said Christopher Robin.

It was Pooh bumping his head against a tree-root he had found.

"There!" said Piglet. "Isn't it *awful?*" And he held on tight to Christopher Robin's hand.

Suddenly Christopher Robin began to laugh . . . and he laughed . . . and he laughed . . . and he laughed. And while he was still laughing—*Crash* went the Heffalump's head against the tree-root, Smash went the jar, and out came Pooh's head again. . . .

Then Piglet saw what a Foolish Piglet he had been, and he was so ashamed of himself that he ran straight off home and went to bed with a headache. But Christopher Robin and Pooh went home to breakfast together.

"Oh, Bear!" said Christopher Robin. "How I do love you!"

"So do I," said Pooh.

◆ LIBRARY LINK ◆

This story was taken from the book Winnie-the-Pooh. *You might enjoy reading the entire book to learn more about Pooh and his friends and all the fun they have together.*

Reader's **Response**

If you could talk with Piglet and Pooh, what questions would you ask them?

Writing a Character Riddle

This unit was about characters who sent and received messages in different ways. A character riddle is a message that asks you to guess who the story character is. The clues are from the story, and you can use those clues to guess the character. The clues are written in the order in which they come in the story.

Here is a character riddle. See if you can figure out who the character is.

◆ I want to run about and kick up my heels.

◆ I want to sleep in a red barn.

◆ I want to sip water from a bubbling brook.

◆ Who am I?

Did you get the message? Did you guess the horse in "The Horse Who Lived Upstairs"? Now you are going to write a character riddle, and your classmates are going to try to solve it.

Prewriting

Choose and draw a favorite character. Then draw five lines next to your character. On each line, write something the character does. This diagram will help you think of clues for your riddle.

Run about.

Want to live in a green meadow.

Kick up my heels.

Want to sip water from a bubbling brook.

Want to sleep in a real barn.

Writing

Choose three interesting details from your diagram. Use the details to write a riddle about the character. Write the clues as if *you* are the character. Put the clues in the same order as they are in the story. End your riddle with the question "Who am I?"

Revising

Read your character riddle to a partner. Can your partner guess which character the riddle is about? If not, add more details to your clues.

Proofreading

Use a dictionary to check your spelling. Be sure you began the first word of each sentence with a capital letter. Make a neat copy of your riddle.

Publishing

Make a character-riddle game with index cards. You and your classmates can try to guess the answers to each other's riddles.

Sending a Message Without Words ▪▪▪▪▪▪▪▪▪▪▪▪▪▪▪▪▪

In this unit you read how coaches send messages to their players without using words. Many people send messages without words. Have you ever seen a police officer directing traffic? Your group will practice sending a message without words.

Group members should do one or more of these tasks:

◆ Look at others when they talk.

◆ Record everyone's ideas on a list.

◆ Ask questions.

◆ Help group members understand what they should do.

Begin by talking about messages you might want to send. You might ask people to do something, go somewhere, or give you something, such as a pencil or a book. Take turns giving ideas for possible messages. Make a list of everyone's ideas. Together, choose one of them. Then discuss how a person could send the message without using words. Everyone should suggest ideas.

Try out the ideas on each other. If the message isn't easy to understand, think of ways to make it clearer. Then talk about when you might use this way of sending messages.

Train Whistles by Helen Roney Sattler *(Lothrop, 1984)* The toots of a train whistle are a way for trains to signal to other trains, from one car of the train to another, and to people. Example: Two long toots, one short, and a long mean, "Stop, cars and people! Wait until the train has passed!"

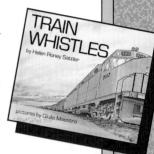

Computers by Jane Jonas Srivastava *(Harper & Row, 1972)* This book explains the basic units common to all computers and the kinds of tasks people program them to do.

The Seeing Stick by Jane Yolen *(Harper & Row, 1977)* This is the Chinese tale of an emperor who is sad because his daughter is blind. An old man says he can help her see with his "seeing stick."

Finger Rhymes by Marc Brown *(Dutton, 1980)* Fourteen familiar rhymes are presented.

◆ 345

GLOSSARY

Full pronunciation key*   The pronunciation of each word is shown just after the word, in this way: **abbreviate** (ə brē′vē āt).

The letters and signs used are pronounced as in the words below.

The mark ′ is placed after a syllable with a primary or heavy accent as in the example above.

The mark ′ after a syllable shows a secondary or lighter accent, as in **abbreviation** (ə brē′vē ā′shən).

SYMBOL	KEY WORDS	SYMBOL	KEY WORDS	SYMBOL	KEY WORDS
a	ask, fat	u	up, cut	r	red, dear
ā	ape, date	ur	fur, fern	s	sell, pass
ä	car, father			t	top, hat
		ə	a in ago	v	vat, have
e	elf, ten		e in agent	w	will, always
er	berry, care		e in father	y	yet, yard
ē	even, meet		i in unity	z	zebra, haze
			o in collect		
i	is, hit		u in focus	ch	chin, arch
ir	mirror, here			ŋ	ring, singer
ī	ice, fire	b	bed, dub	sh	she, dash
		d	did, had	th	thin, truth
o	lot, pond	f	fall, off	*th*	then, father
ō	open, go	g	get, dog	zh	s in pleasure
ô	law, horn	h	he, ahead		
oi	oil, point	j	joy, jump	′	as in (ā′b′l)
oo	look, pull	k	kill, bake		
ōō	ooze, tool	l	let, ball		
yoo	unite, cure	m	met, trim		
yōo	cute, few	n	not, ton		
ou	out, crowd	p	put, tap		

*Pronunciation key and respellings adapted from *Webster's New World Dictionary, Basic School Edition*, Copyright © 1983 by Simon & Schuster, Inc. Reprinted by permission.

A

a·board (ə bôrd′) *adverb.* on, in, or into a boat, train, airplane, or bus.

ab·so·lute·ly (ab′sə lōōt lē) *adverb.* completely; perfectly.

ac·tor (ak′tər) *noun.* a person, especially a boy or man, who performs in plays, in movies, or on television. **actors.**

ad·ven·ture (əd ven′chər) *noun.* **1.** a dangerous event. **2.** an unusual or exciting experience.

ad·vice (əd vīs′) *noun.* an opinion given about what action to take or about how to do something.

al·pha·bet (al′fə bet) *noun.* **1.** the letters of a language placed in order. **2.** a system of symbols used in communicating, such as the Braille alphabet for the blind.

am·ble (am′b′l) *verb.* **1.** to walk in a slow, easy way. **2.** to move slowly and smoothly by raising both legs on one side, then both legs on the other side; used to describe the way a horse, donkey, etc., moves. **ambled.**

an·chor (ang′kər) *noun.* a heavy object that is lowered into the water on a rope or chain to keep a boat from drifting, usually a metal piece with hooks that dig into the ground under the water.

an·nounce (ə nouns′) *verb.* **1.** to say or tell something to an audience. **2.** to make something known to others: He *announced* that the class would take a trip to the museum. **3.** to say or tell. **announced.**

at·ten·tion (ə ten′shən) *noun.* the ability to keep your mind or thoughts on something; notice.

awk·ward (ôk′wərd) *adjective.* **1.** not moving in a graceful way; clumsy. **2.** difficult to use or hold: It was *awkward* to carry so many packages.

ax·le (ak′s′l) *noun.* a bar or rod on which the wheels at each end turn: When the *axle* broke on the wagon, one wheel rolled down the hill.

aboard

Alphabet is taken from two Greek words *alpha* and *beta*. These two words are the names of the first two letters in the Greek alphabet.

axle

B

Ballet is a French word that became part of the English language. Ballet started in France three hundred years ago. When it spread to England, people used the French word for the new style of dance.

breeches

bugle

bab·ble (bab″l) *verb.* **1.** to make sounds like talking that are not understood by others; baby talk. **2.** to chatter or talk fast. **3.** to speak foolishly. —**babbling** *adjective.* bubbling or gurgling sounds, like water running over stones: The deer drank water from the *babbling* brook.

bal·let (bal′ā *or* ba lā′) *noun.* a dance that tells a story through a series of planned, graceful movements usually performed by dancers wearing costumes.

beak (bēk) *noun.* **1.** the bill of a bird, especially of an eagle, a hawk, or another bird of prey. **2.** anything that looks like a bird's beak.

be·lief (bə lēf′) *noun.* **1.** a thought or feeling that something is true or real; faith. **2.** anything accepted as true. **beliefs.**

blub·ber (blub′ər) *noun.* fat under the skins of seals, whales, and other sea animals.

bore (bôr) *verb.* to tire by being dull or uninteresting. —**boring** *adjective.* dull, uninteresting.

bor·row (bor′ō *or* bôr′ō) *verb.* **1.** to use something that belongs to someone else after agreeing to return it. **2.** to use someone else's ideas, ways of doing things, etc., as your own. **borrowed.**

breech·es (brich′iz) *plural noun.* short pants that stop just below the knees.

bu·gle (byōō′g′l) *noun.* a type of small trumpet, usually without playing keys or valves.

bunk (buṇk) *noun.* **1.** a built-in bed that hangs on a wall like a shelf. **2.** a narrow bed: The cowboy went to his *bunk* after a hard day's work.

bunt (bunt) *verb.* to bat a baseball lightly so that it does not go beyond the infield.

busi·ness (biz′nis) *noun.* **1.** work that someone does to earn money. **2.** a place where work is done or things are made or sold. **3.** a matter or affair: The girls met to make rules and talk about other club *business.*

C

ca·ble (kā′b′l) *noun.* **1.** a strong rope, usually made of covered wires or metal twisted together. **2.** a bundle of insulated wires that conduct electricity. **3.** a shorter word for *cablegram,* a telegraph message sent overseas.

cham·ber (chām′bər) *noun.* **1.** a room, usually a bedroom. **2.** a large room used for meetings, such as an assembly hall.

charm (chärm) *noun.* **1.** something believed to have magical powers, either good or evil. **2.** a small object on a bracelet or necklace. **3.** a physical feature or a personal characteristic that is pleasing, delightful, or attractive.

chat·ter (chat′ər) *verb.* **1.** to make short, quick noises that sound like talking: The birds were *chattering* outside the window. **2.** to talk fast and foolishly without stopping. **chattering.**

chick·en (chik′ən) *noun.* **1.** a young hen or rooster. **2.** the meat of a chicken. **chickens.**

choice (chois) *noun.* **1.** the act of choosing or picking. **2.** having the chance, power, or right to choose. **3.** someone or something chosen.

choke (chōk) *verb.* **1.** to try to breathe when something is stuck in the windpipe. **2.** to squeeze the throat to stop breathing. **3.** to have trouble breathing. **choked.**

chore (chôr) *noun.* **1.** the regular light work such as that done at home or on a farm: His *chores* on the farm include feeding the chickens. **2.** a task that is difficult or uninteresting. **chores.**

clam·ber (klam′bər) *verb.* to climb by trying hard, especially using both the hands and feet: The boy *clambered* up the tree. **clambered.**

clerk (klurk) *noun.* **1.** a person who sells in a store. **2.** an office worker who keeps records and types letters.

cli·mate (klī′mət) *noun.* the typical weather of a place, year after year: In some cold *climates* people wear coats all year long. **climates.**

cob·ble·stone (kob″l stōn) *noun.* a rounded stone that was used to pave the streets long ago. **cobblestones.**

a fat	oi oil	ch chin
ā ape	oo look	sh she
ä car, father	o͞o tool	th thin
e ten	ou out	th then
er care	u up	zh leisure
ē even	ur fur	ŋ ring
i hit		
ir here	ə = a *in* ago	
ī bite, fire	e *in* agent	
o lot	i *in* unity	
ō go	o *in* collect	
ô law, horn	u *in* focus	

chicken

Cobblestone is made up of *cobble* and *stone*. *Cob* is a very old word meaning "plump" or "round."

com·mu·ni·cate
(kə my$\overline{oo}$′nə kāt) *verb.* to make something known to others; to give or share information: Long ago, some Native Americans could *communicate* by sending smoke signals.

com·plain (kəm plān′) *verb.* to tell about or show pain or unhappiness about something.

con·cen·trate (kon′sən trāt) *verb.* to focus all your attention on something: He will *concentrate* on learning how to play the piano.

con·gress·man (kän͡g′ grəs mən) *noun.* an elected official who votes on laws in Congress. **congressmen.**

con·sid·er (kən sid′ər) *verb.*
1. to think about something in order to make a decision.
2. to keep something in mind while making a decision or in taking an action. **3.** to believe something about someone. **considering.**

coun·cil (koun′s′l) *noun.* **1.** a group of people who meet to make plans or decisions.
2. a group of people elected to make the laws for a town.

cour·age (kʉr′ij) *noun.* the ability to control fear in order to go through danger, pain, or trouble; bravery.

croc·o·dile (krok′ə dīl) *noun.* a large tropical lizard like an alligator, with thick skin, a long tail, a long, narrow, triangular head with large jaws, and cone-shaped teeth.

cun·ning (kun′in͡g) *adjective.* clever; able to cheat or trick others: The *cunning* fox was able to fool the rabbit.

cus·to·mer (kus′tə mər) *noun.* a person who buys, often again and again, from the same place. **customers.**

crocodile

dawn

D

dan·gle (dan͡g′g′l) *verb.* to hang loosely so as to swing. **dangled.**

dawn (dôn) *verb.* **1.** to begin to be day; to grow light.
2. to begin to happen.
—*noun.* the first light of day.

deaf (def) *adjective.* **1.** not able to hear or not able to hear well. **2.** not wanting to hear or listen.

de·ci·sion (di sizh′ən) *noun.* the act of making up your mind about something, or the choice decided on: He made a *decision* about what to wear.

deck (dek) *noun.* **1.** the floor of a ship. **2.** a pack of 52 playing cards.

de·pend (di pend′) *verb.* **1.** to trust someone to give help. **2.** to be determined by something or someone else: The amount of snowfall varies, *depending* on where you live. **depending.**

de·serve (di zʉrv′) *verb.* to have the right to something: We worked hard and we *deserve* the prize.

des·ti·na·tion (des′tə nā′shən) *noun.* the place where someone is going.

de·ter·mined (di tʉr′mənd) *adjective.* **1.** having your mind made up. **2.** strong and sure.

dif·fi·cult (dif′i kəlt) *adjective.* **1.** hard to do or make; causing a lot of trouble, thought, time, or practice; hard to understand. **2.** hard to get along with.

dis·con·tent·ed (dis′kən tent′id) *adjective.* not satisfied; wanting something different.

dis·o·bey (dis ə bā′) *verb.* to refuse to follow orders.

dis·please (dis plēz′) *verb.* to anger or dissatisfy; to be bothered by: They were *displeased* by the long lines of people outside the store. **displeased.**

dis·tance (dis′təns) *noun.* **1.** the amount of space between two points. **2.** a place far away.

dis·tress (dis tres′) *verb.* to cause worry, sorrow, or trouble. —*noun.* worry; pain; unhappiness.

dive (dīv) *verb.* **1.** to plunge headfirst into water. **2.** to go underwater to look for something. **3.** to move or drop suddenly. **dived.**

dol·phin (dol′fən) *noun.* a water animal belonging to the same family as the whale, but smaller than the whale. **dolphins.**

drawn (drôn) *verb.* to be pulled: The wagon was *drawn* by two horses.

a fat	oi oil	ch chin
ā ape	oo look	sh she
ä car, father	o͞o tool	th thin
e ten	ou out	*th* then
er care	u up	zh leisure
ē even	ur fur	nĝ ring
i hit		
ir here	ə = a *in* ago	
ī bite, fire	e *in* agent	
o lot	i *in* unity	
ō go	o *in* collect	
ô law, horn	u *in* focus	

deck

E

ea·ger (ē′gər) *adjective.* wanting very much to do or get something.

ech·o (ek′ō) *noun.* a sound heard again after it bounces off a surface. —*verb.* to repeat.

dolphin

351

ed·i·tor (ed′ə tər) *noun.* a person in charge of putting together a newspaper or magazine.

ed·u·ca·tion (ej′ə kā′shən) *noun.* what you learn by being taught in school or by training.

el·e·va·tor (el′ə vāt′ər) *noun.* a platform or box that moves up and down in a shaft and that carries people and things between floors in buildings.

em·bar·rass (im ber′əs) *verb.* to make feel uncomfortable or uneasy. —**embarrassed** *adjective.* self-conscious; ashamed.

emp·ty (emp′tē) *adjective.* having nothing inside. —*verb.* to take everything out of a jar, bottle, etc.

en·gi·neer (en′jə nir′) *noun.* a person who is trained to plan and build machines, roads, bridges, etc. **engineers.**

Eng·lish (iñg′glish) *adjective.* of England, its language, or its people.

es·pe·cial·ly (ə spesh′əl ē) *adverb.* mostly; in particular: I like candy, *especially* chocolate.

ex·it (eg′zit *or* ek′sit) *noun.* a way out of a place, such as a door. —*verb.* to go out; to leave.

Elevator comes from a Latin word that means "to lighten" or "raise up."

engineer

Farmhand is a compound word made up of *farm* and *hand.* *Hand* in this case refers to a person who works with his or her hands.

F

fame (fām) *noun.* known by many people through books, television, newspapers, etc.

fa·mil·iar (fə mil′yər) *adjective.* **1.** close; friendly; knowing someone or something well. **2.** acting too friendly in a pushy way. **3.** ordinary or usual.

farm·hand (färm′hand) *noun.* a person who works on a farm to earn money. **farmhands.**

fault (fôlt) *noun.* **1.** a thing or problem that keeps something or someone from being perfect. He has many *faults,* but he is still my friend. **2.** a mistake. **3.** being the cause of something unwanted. **faults.**

fa·vor·ite (fā′vər it) *noun.* a person or thing that is liked better than others. —*adjective.* best liked; preferred.

fend·er (fen′dər) *noun.* a metal piece over each wheel of a car that protects the car from mud, stones, etc. **fenders.**

fib·er·glass (fī′bər glas′) *noun.* material made of glass threads that is used to make cloth, insulation, boats, etc.

fish·er·man (fish'ər mən) *noun.* someone who catches or tries to catch fish for sport or for a living. **fishermen.**

flake (flāk) *noun.* a small, thin, usually flat piece of something.

flip·per (flip'ər) *noun.* **1.** the wide, flat body part on seals, whales, etc., used for swimming. **2.** a wide, flat rubber shoe that swimmers wear to help them move through water. **flippers.**

flock (flok) *noun.* a group of animals or birds that eat and travel together.

flut·ter (flut'ər) *verb.* **1.** to flap the wings quickly in a short flight or without flying. **2.** to move with quick motions. **fluttered.**

fore·cast·er (fôr'kast ər) *noun.* someone who tries to predict how events will turn out.

freight train (frāt trān) *noun.* a train that carries a load of goods. **freight trains.**

fu·ture (fyo͞o'chər) *noun.* a time that is to come: In the *future,* I will study more for tests.

G

gal·ley (gal'ē) *noun.* **1.** a long, low ship used long ago, moved by sails and oars. **2.** the kitchen of a boat or ship: The sailor went to the *galley* to start cooking.

ga·losh·es (gə losh'iz) *plural noun.* overshoes that come high above the ankles, worn in wet or snowy weather.

gar·ment (gär'mənt) *noun.* a piece of clothing, such as a skirt, a pair of pants, etc. **garments.**

glit·ter (glit'ər) *verb.* to shine with a sparkling light. **glittered.**

gloom·i·ly (glo͞om'ə lē) *adverb.* very sadly; in a deeply unhappy way.

goal (gōl) *noun.* **1.** the destination at the end of a race or trip. **2.** a purpose toward which one's actions are aimed: Their *goal* was to finish cleaning the house before the guests arrived. **3.** a net, line, or pocket over or into which a ball must go for a team or player to score in certain games.

a fat	oi oil	ch chin
ā ape	o͝o look	sh she
ä car, father	o͞o tool	th thin
e ten	ou out	*th* then
er care	u up	zh leisure
ē even	ur fur	ng ring
i hit		
ir here	ə = a *in* ago	
ī bite, fire	e *in* agent	
o lot	i *in* unity	
ō go	o *in* collect	
ô law, horn	u *in* focus	

flock

Galoshes used to be a kind of high wooden sandal. These sandals were worn over shoes to keep a person's feet out of the mud. Today galoshes do the same thing, but they are made of rubber, not wood.

353

H

hes·i·tate (hez′ə tāt) *verb.* **1.** to stop or hold back for a moment as if feeling unsure. **2.** to feel unwilling to do something. **hesitated.**

hike (hīk) *noun.* a long walk, especially through the woods or in the countryside.

hon·or (on′ər) *noun.* **1.** a sign of respect: It was an *honor* to be chosen for the advanced class. **2.** credit or glory, as in winning a prize. **3.** good name.

hood (hood) *noun.* **1.** a piece that covers the head and neck, often attached to a jacket or coat. **2.** a metal cover in the front of an automobile over the engine.

hoot owl (hoot oul) *noun.* a bird with a large head, large eyes, small hooked beak, and sharp claws. It makes a long, low sound.

horn (hôrn) *noun.* **1.** a musical instrument played by blowing. **2.** a device that makes a loud, warning noise.

house·hold (hous′hōld) *noun.* all the people who live in a house, especially a family.

hug (hug) *verb.* **1.** to put the arms around and hold close in a loving way. **2.** to keep close. **hugging.**

hur·ri·cane (hur′ə kān) *noun.* a storm with strong winds blowing in a circle at 73 miles per hour or more, usually with heavy rains.

I

ice·berg (īs′burg) *noun.* a huge piece of ice, floating in the sea; most of an iceberg is under the water.

i·cy (ī′sē) *adjective.* **1.** covered with ice; frozen or slippery. **2.** feeling very cold like ice.

ig·nore (ig nôr′) *verb.* to act as if something is not happening: Try to *ignore* the noises from the street and just keep talking.

in·clude (in klood′) *verb.* to take something in as a part of a whole or group: Will you *include* this in the box?

in·ning (in′ ing) *noun.* a part of a baseball game in which both teams get a turn at bat; there are usually nine innings in a baseball game.

in·sist (in sist′) *verb.* **1.** to demand in a stubborn or strong way. **2.** to stick to an idea strongly.

hood

hoot owl

Hoot is a good example of a word that is taken directly from a sound. The word *hoot* in *hoot owl* sounds like the call of an owl.

354

in·stru·ment (in′strə mənt) *noun.* **1.** a tool or machine used to do exact work: The doctor always washed his *instruments* after he used them. **2.** something on which music can be played, such as a drum, violin, flute, etc. **instruments.**

in·ter·rupt (in tə rupt′) *verb.* **1.** to make a break in something, as in someone talking: He *interrupted* the lesson when he came late to class. **2.** to keep something from going on; to cut off. **interrupted.**

in·tro·duce (in trə do͞os′ *or* in trə dyo͞os′) *verb.* to present or make known to others. **introduces.**

in·vi·ta·tion (in′və ta′shən) *noun.* **1.** the act of inviting a person to go somewhere or do something. **2.** the spoken or written way of inviting.

J

jun·gle (jung′g′l) *noun.* land in warm, moist parts of the world, covered with trees, plants, and vines.

K

key·board (kē′bôrd) *noun.* **1.** the row or rows of black and white keys on a piano or organ. **2.** the lettered and numbered keys on a computer or typewriter.

kind·ness (kīnd′nis) *noun.* the habit or way of being friendly, good, generous, etc., to others.

L

lad·en (lād″n) *adjective.* having or carrying a heavy load: Mother left the department store *laden* with packages.

lan·guage (lang′gwij) *noun.* **1.** the speech or writing people use to understand each other. **2.** any way of communicating thoughts or feelings, such as the way sign language uses hand gestures to mean words. **3.** the written or spoken words of a certain group of people: My pen pal speaks English as well as the Korean *language.*

a fat	oi oil	ch chin
ā ape	o͞o look	sh she
ä car, father	o͞o tool	th thin
e ten	ou out	*th* then
er care	u up	zh leisure
ē even	ur fur	ng ring
i hit		
ir here	ə = a *in* ago	
ī bite, fire	e *in* agent	
o lot	i *in* unity	
ō go	o *in* collect	
ô law, horn	u *in* focus	

keyboard

laden

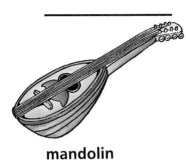

mandolin

Marathon races are so named because of a messenger in Greece over two thousand years ago. This messenger ran 26 miles from a city named Marathon to the city of Athens. He delivered the message that the Greeks had defeated the Persians in battle. Modern marathons are the same distance that the ancient messenger ran.

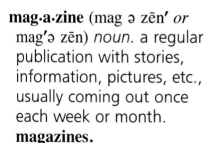

medal

li·brar·y (lī'brer'ē) *noun.* a place where a collection of books, magazines, records, or films is kept for reading or borrowing.

lit·er·ar·y (lit'ə rer'ē) *adjective.* **1.** having to do with the written work of a country, a time in history, etc., that people enjoy reading. **2.** having to do with writing.

lull (lul) *verb.* **1.** to make or become calm or quiet. **2.** to calm by using soft sounds or movements. **lulled.**

lung (lung) *noun.* one of the two organs in the chest used to breathe: The mountain climber took a deep breath and filled his *lungs* with fresh air. **lungs.**

M

mag·a·zine (mag ə zēn' *or* mag'ə zēn) *noun.* a regular publication with stories, information, pictures, etc., usually coming out once each week or month. **magazines.**

main·land (mān' land *or* mān' lənd) *noun.* the greatest part of a country or continent; not an island.

mam·mal (mam'əl) *noun.* any of a group of animals where the females have special glands that produce milk to feed their young. **mammals.**

man·age (man'ij) *verb.* **1.** to be in charge of. **2.** to be sure that things get done in workplaces, homes, etc. **3.** to succeed in doing something: She *managed* to swim across the lake. **managed.**

man·do·lin (man'd'l in) *noun.* a musical instrument with eight or ten strings played with a pick.

man·go (mang'gō) *noun.* **1.** a tropical fruit with a yellowish-red thick skin and a hard stone inside. **2.** the tree on which this fruit grows.

mar·a·thon (mar'ə thon) *noun.* a race run on foot, about 26 miles long.

may·or (mā'ər *or* mer) *noun.* the person elected by the people of a city or town to be in charge of its government.

med·al (med"l) *noun.* a piece of metal with words or pictures on it, usually given as a prize to people who do something special.

mem·o·ry (mem'ər ē) *noun.*
1. the act of remembering things. **2.** anything that someone remembers: Her good *memories* of summer camp gave her pleasure all winter long. **3.** the part of a computer that stores information. **memories.**

mes·quite (mes kēt' *or* mes'kēt) *noun.* a kind of tree or shrub with thorns and sugary, beanlike pods that are often used to feed animals.

mes·sen·ger (mes''n jər) *noun.* a person who carries mail or things from one place to another: The *messenger* took the package and delivered it to the bank.

me·te·or·ol·o·gy (mēt'ē ə rol'ə jē) *noun.* the study or science of weather.

mil·let (mil'it) *noun.* **1.** a kind of grass grown for hay. **2.** the seeds of this grass, or grain, as used as food in some parts of the world.

mil·lion (mil'yən) *noun.* one thousand thousands (1,000,000). **millions.**

min·is·ter (min'is tər) *noun.* the head of a church, especially a Protestant church; a religious leader. **ministers.**

min·now (min' ō) *noun.* a very small fish.

mis·chief (mis'chif) *noun.*
1. harm, damage, or injury.
2. an act that causes harm.
3. a person, especially a child, who bothers people or things. **4.** playful tricks: He is always getting into *mischief* when his mother is busy.

mis·take (mi stāk') *noun.* something done incorrectly or in error.

mix·ture (miks'chər) *noun.* something made by blending different things into a single, whole thing.

mor·sel (môr' s'l) *noun.* a small bit of food.

most·ly (môst'lē) *adverb.* for the greater part; mainly.

mous·tache (mə stash *or* mus' tash) *noun.* the hair a man has let grow out on his upper lip.

move·ment (mo͞ov'mənt) *noun.* the act of moving or changing place.

mule (myo͞ol) *noun.* **1.** an animal whose parents are a horse and a donkey. **2.** a person who is stubborn. *used only in informal language.*

mus·cle (mus''l) *noun.* the tissue in the body that stretches and tightens to move the body. **muscles.**

a fat	oi oil	ch chin
ā ape	o͝o look	sh she
ä car, father	o͞o tool	th thin
e ten	ou out	*th* then
er care	u up	zh leisure
ē even	ur fur	n̄g ring
i hit		
ir here	ə = a *in* ago	
ī bite, fire	e *in* agent	
o lot	i *in* unity	
ō go	o *in* collect	
ô law, horn	u *in* focus	

millet

mule

mus·tang (mus′tang̃) *noun.* a small, wild horse that usually runs free in some parts of the southwestern United States. **mustangs.**

mustang

nuz·zle (nuz″l) *verb.* **1.** to rub with the nose: The dog *nuzzled* the puppy. **2.** to lie close and be comfortable. **nuzzled.**

N

na·ture (nā′chər) *noun.* **1.** the universe and everything in it that is not made by humans. **2.** the outdoors, including plants, animals, flowers, etc.

ne·glect (ni glekt′) *verb.* **1.** not to take care of as one should: He *neglected* to walk the dog yesterday. **2.** to take little notice of. **neglected.**

neigh·bor·hood (nā′bər hood) *noun.* **1.** a small part of a city, town, etc.: My school is in my *neighborhood.* **2.** people who live near each other.

nib·ble (nib″l) *verb.* **1.** to eat quickly in small bites. **2.** to bite carefully.

note (nōt) *noun.* **1.** a word or sentence written to help you remember something. **2.** a short letter. **3.** a musical tone or the symbol that stands for a musical tone as written on paper. **notes.**

nuzzle

O

of·fi·cial (ə fish′əl) *noun.* **1.** a person who holds office, usually in government. **2.** a person who makes sure that the rules are followed in sports. —*adjective.* coming from someone in authority.

out·field·er (out′fēl′dər) *noun.* a baseball player who stays in center, left, or right field. **outfielders.**

o·val (ō′v′l) *adjective.* having a shape like an egg.

P

pause (pôz) *noun.* to break for a moment when talking; stop for a moment.

perch (purch) *verb.* to rest, as on a place where a bird sits: The eagle *perched* on the rooftop. **perched.**

perch

per·form·ance (pər fôr′məns) *noun.* the act of doing something before an audience.

per·for·mer (pər fôr′mər) *noun.* a person who acts, plays an instrument, or shows another skill before an audience. **performers.**

per·suade (pər swād′) *verb.* to get someone to act or think in a certain way by making it seem like a good thing.

pi·an·o (pē an′ō) *noun.* a large musical instrument with wire strings in a case and a keyboard.

pic·nic (pik′nik) *verb.* to go on an outing that includes eating a meal outdoors. **picnicking.**

pil·grim (pil′grəm) *noun.* **1.** a person who travels to places away from home for religious reasons. **2. Pilgrim.** one of the group of Puritans who left England and settled in Plymouth, Massachusetts, in 1620. **Pilgrims.**

pi·lot (pī′lət) *noun.* **1.** a person who steers a ship. **2.** a person who flies an airplane or helicopter.

pitch·er (pich′ər) *noun.* a baseball player who throws the ball so the batters can try to hit it.

plan·et (plan′it) *noun.* a large heavenly body that moves in an orbit or path around a star.

plow (plou) *noun.* a farm tool, pulled by an animal or a tractor, that breaks up the soil into rows to get it ready for planting.

plug (plug) *verb.* **1.** to close up a hole. **2.** to work hard and steadily at something: When we came home, the workers were still *plugging* away at digging the trench. **plugging.**

plunge (plunj) *verb.* **1.** to throw or push with great power. **2.** to dive. **plunged.**

pock·et (pok′it) *noun.* a small bag or pouch sewn into clothing and used to hold things. **pockets.**

po·em (pō′əm) *noun.* a written work that uses a pattern of sounds, tempo, and words that rhyme to show an idea or experience that is deeply felt by the writer.

po·et·ry (pō′ə trē) *noun.* **1.** the art of writing poems. **2.** poems.

po·lice·man (pə lēs′mən) *noun.* a member of the police department.

a fat	**oi** oil	**ch** chin
ā ape	**oo** look	**sh** she
ä car, father	**ōō** tool	**th** thin
e ten	**ou** out	**th** then
er care	**u** up	**zh** leisure
ē even	**ur** fur	**ŋ** ring
i hit		
ir here	**ə** = a *in* ago	
ī bite, fire	e *in* agent	
o lot	i *in* unity	
ō go	o *in* collect	
ô law, horn	u *in* focus	

piano

Piano comes from the Italian word, *pianoforte*, which means "soft" and "strong." The inventor of the piano chose this name because the new instrument could be played both softly and loudly.

practice

punt

pop·u·lar (pop′yə lər) *adjective.* **1.** being well liked by many people. **2.** something that is liked by a lot of people.

pop·u·lar·i·ty (pop′yə lar′ə tē) *noun.* the state of being well liked.

po·si·tion (pə zish′ən) *noun.* **1.** the way a person or thing is placed. **2.** the place where a person or thing is, especially how near or far from other things. **3.** a job that someone does.

prac·tice (prak′tis) *verb.* **1.** to make a habit of doing something regularly. **2.** to repeat an action in order to become skilled.

pre·dic·tion (pri dik′shən) *noun.* trying to tell what will happen in the future.

prep·a·ra·tion (prep′ə rā′shən) *noun.* **1.** getting or being ready for something. **2.** doing things to get ready. **preparations.**

pre·pare (pri par′) *verb.* **1.** to make or get ready: He can't go with us because he has to *prepare* for a test. **2.** to put something together.

press (pres) *noun.* **1.** a machine that prints pages from inked type, plates, or rolls: The newspaper was printed on a *press.* **2.** a machine that smooths or squeezes something. **3.** newspapers and magazines or the people who work for them. **presses.**

print (print) *verb.* **1.** to press letters or designs onto a surface. **2.** to produce writing to be sold. **3.** to write in letters similar to those in books. **printed.**

pro·vide (prə vīd′) *verb.* **1.** to give what is needed. **2.** to support. **3.** to get ready ahead of time. **provided.**

pub·lish (pub′lish) *verb.* to get a book, magazine, newspaper, etc., printed and brought to market for sale. **published.**

punt (punt) *noun.* the act of kicking a football after it is dropped from the hands but before it hits the ground.

purr (pŭr) *verb.* to make the soft sound a cat makes when it is happy. **purred.**

R

rack·et (rak′it) *verb.* to make a loud, clattering noise. **racketing.**

ra·di·o (rā′dē o′) *noun.* **1.** a way that sounds are sent from one place to another by changing them into electrical waves that travel through the air. **2.** a receiving set that picks up those waves and changes them back into sounds.

raw (rô) *adjective.* **1.** uncooked. **2.** in its natural state. **3.** uncomfortably cold and damp: The *raw* wind made us return home early.

re·ci·tal (ri sīt″l) *noun.* **1.** the act of telling every part of a story. **2.** a story told like this. **3.** a music or dance program where people perform on stage alone or in a small group.

re·cov·er (ri kuv′ər) *verb.* **1.** to get back something that was lost. **2.** to get well again after being sick: I am sure that she will *recover* soon from her bad cold.

re·frig·er·a·tor (ri frij′ə rāt′or) *noun.* a machine or room that keeps food, drinks, etc., cold and fresh.

re·lax (ri laks′) *verb.* **1.** to make something loose. **2.** to rest after working or doing something.

re·lief (ri lēf′) *noun.* freedom from pain, worry, or uncomfortable feelings: We were worried, but it is a *relief* to know you are safe.

re·li·gion (ri lij′ən) *noun.* **1.** a belief in God or gods. **2.** a way of living by worshipping God.

re·li·gious (re lij′əs) *adjective.* **1.** showing belief in God or a religion. **2.** having to do with religion.

re·mind (ri mīnd′) *verb.* to make or help someone remember; to tell something to someone again: He *reminded* me that we had a date. **reminded.**

re·ply (ri plī′) *verb.* to answer in words or in actions: Susan *replied* to his letter right away. **replied.**

re·ward (ri wôrd′) *noun.* **1.** something given in return for good work. **2.** money given for finding and returning something that was lost.

S

scene (sēn) *noun.* the place and time of a play or story.

a fat	oi oil	ch chin
ā ape	oo look	sh she
ä car, father	ōō tool	th thin
e ten	ou out	th then
er care	u up	zh leisure
ē even	ur fur	ŋ ring
i hit		
ir here	ə = a *in* ago	
ī bite, fire	e *in* agent	
o lot	i *in* unity	
ō go	o *in* collect	
ô law, horn	u *in* focus	

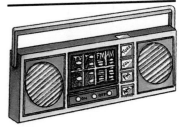

radio

relax

sched·ule (skej'ool) *noun.* **1.** a list of times at which things will happen; timetable. **2.** a list of things to be done with time limits given in which those things must be done.

schol·ar (skol'ər) *noun.* **1.** a person who learns a lot by studying. **2.** a person who goes to school or studies with a teacher. **3.** a student who enjoys study and learning.

sci·en·tist (sī'ən tist) *noun.* a person who is an expert in a particular branch of science, such as biology, agriculture, etc. **scientists.**

scold (skōld) *verb.* to tell someone what he or she is doing wrong in an angry voice: He *scolded* me for arriving late for class. **scolded.**

seal (sēl) *noun.* a sea animal having four flippers that lives in cold waters and is covered with fur. **seals.**

sep·a·rate (sep'ə rāt) *verb.* **1.** to set apart. **2.** to put something between other things. **3.** to go away from one another. —**separated** *adjective.* set apart; divided.

se·ri·ous (sir'ē əs) *adjective.* **1.** having thoughts that are deeply felt; important. **2.** not joking or fooling around;

sincere: John is *serious* about completing his project on time.

serv·ant (sur'vənt) *noun.* someone who is paid to work in another person's home as cook, butler, maid, etc.

shaft (shaft) *noun.* **1.** the long, thin part of an arrow or spear. **2.** a handle. **3.** one of the two long pieces of wood between which an animal pulls a wagon, plow, etc. **4.** a long tunnel dug into the earth, like a mine shaft. **5.** a long opening that goes through the floors of a building, such as for an elevator. **shafts.**

shim·mer (shim'ər) *verb.* to shine with a wavering kind of light: The puddle of water on the sidewalk was *shimmering* under the street light. **shimmering.**

ship·wreck (ship'rek) *noun.* the parts of a ship left after it is destroyed or lost at sea.

shiv·er (shiv'ər) *verb.* to shake as when you are very cold or afraid; to tremble. **shivered.**

short·stop (shôrt'stop) *noun.* a baseball player who fields the balls hit between second and third base.

shipwreck

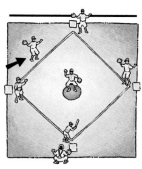
shortstop

sigh (sī) *noun.* a long, deep breathing sound made when sad, tired, or relieved. **sighs.**

sign (sīn) *noun.* a word, picture, or action that tells of something else. —*verb.* using a part of the body to show or mean something, as in nodding the head, waving the hand, etc. **signs.**

sign language *noun.* a system of hand gestures used to talk with people who are deaf.

slave (slāv) *noun.* **1.** a person owned by someone else. **2.** a person who is controlled by something else.

so·nar (sō'när) *noun.* a machine that sends sound waves through water, to locate objects; used to find submarines, measure the depth of the ocean, etc.

sort (sôrt) *noun.* **1.** a group of things that have something that is the same. **2.** type or kind: There are many *sorts* of toys in the store. **sorts.**

spar·kle (spär'k'l) *verb.* to shine as if giving off sparks or flashes of light.

sput·ter (sput'ər) *verb.* **1.** to spit out food or water from your mouth when speaking. **2.** to talk in a fast, excited way. **3.** to make hissing or popping noises. **sputtered.**

stage (stāj) *noun.* the raised platform in a theater on which actors and entertainers perform.

stall (stôl) *noun.* a space for one animal in a stable or barn.

stal·lion (stal'yən) *noun.* a full-grown male horse that can have offspring: The wild *stallion* galloped across the plains.

stub·born·ly (stub'ərn lē) *adverb.* in a very determined way; in a way that shows unwillingness to listen or to change one's mind: He acted *stubbornly* even after he knew he was wrong.

sub·ma·rine (sub'mə rēn) *noun.* a kind of ship that travels underwater and is able to stay there for a long time.

suf·fer (suf'ər) *verb.* **1.** to feel pain; be uncomfortable. **2.** to put up with problems, pain, worry, etc.

sug·gest (səg jest') *verb.* to bring to mind as something to consider or think over.

sur·round·ings (sə roun'diñgz) *plural noun.* the things that are around a person or around a place: The children did their classwork in beautiful *surroundings.*

a fat	oi oil	ch chin
ā ape	၀၀ look	sh she
ä car, father	ōo tool	th thin
e ten	ou out	th then
er care	u up	zh leisure
ē even	ur fur	ñg ring
i hit		
ir here	ə = a *in* ago	
ī bite, fire	e *in* agent	
o lot	i *in* unity	
ō go	o *in* collect	
ô law, horn	u *in* focus	

Sonar is an acronym. An acronym is a word which is made by putting together the first letters of a longer name or description. Sonar comes from *sound navagation ranging.*

submarine

363

Television is a new word, when compared to most of the words we use. It came into use seventy years ago, when television was first being developed. The word means "seeing at a distance."

throat

trough

sur·vive (sər vīv′) *verb.* to stay alive under bad conditions.

sus·pi·cious (sə spish′əs) *adjective.* **1.** thinking something is wrong without knowing for sure. **2.** questioning whether you can be sure about something.

T

tal·ent (tal′ənt) *noun.* a special ability that a person has from birth.

tel·e·vi·sion (tel′ə vizh′ən) *noun.* **1.** a way of sending pictures from one place to another by changing them into electrical waves that travel through the air. **2.** a receiving set that picks up those waves and changes them back into pictures.

tem·per (tem′pər) *noun.* **1.** the way you feel; mood. **2.** anger: She has quite a *temper;* she yelled at everybody.

thee (*th*ē) *pronoun.* you, as used long ago.

thrash (*th*rash) *verb.* **1.** to hit with a stick, whip, or other object. **2.** to move around wildly or without control: The fish *thrashed* around in the shallow water. **thrashed.**

throat (*th*rōt) *noun.* **1.** the front of the neck. **2.** the part of the neck through which air, food, and water pass from the mouth to the stomach or lungs.

thump (*th*ump) *noun.* **1.** a blow or hit made by something heavy. **2.** the sound made by such a blow.

thy (*th*ī) *pronoun.* your, as used long ago.

ti·tled (tīt″ld) *adjective.* **1.** having a special title such as lord, knight, lady, etc. **2.** having a title or name such as the name of a book.

tour·isty (tŏŏr′ istē) *adjective.* about people who travel for pleasure. *used only in informal language.*

tre·men·dous (tri men′dəs) *adjective.* **1.** very large or huge. **2.** surprisingly wonderful, amazing, etc.

trough (trôf) *noun.* a long rectangular container often used to feed or water animals.

V

val·or (val′ər) *noun.* courage or bravery.

W

warm-blood·ed (wôrm′blud′id) *adjective.* having a body temperature that stays the same, despite the surroundings.

wasp (wosp *or* wôsp) *noun.* a flying insect, with a slender body and a narrow waist, that stings. **wasps.**

wa·ter·fall (wôt′ər fôl) *noun.* a natural stream of water that falls from a high place such as a cliff.

weap·on (wep′ən) *noun.* something used for fighting such as a club, gun, etc. **weapons.**

wea·ther vane (weth′ər vān′) *noun.* a device that turns in the wind to show which way the wind is blowing, often placed on a rooftop.

webbed (webd) *adjective.* having the toes joined by pieces of skin or flesh: Ducks have *webbed* feet.

week·ly (wēk′lē) *adjective.* happening or appearing once a week or every week.

wharf (hwôrf) *noun.* a long platform built from the shore out over the water so that ships can be loaded and unloaded.

wheel·ing (hwēl′iṅg) *verb.* turning around in a circular motion.

whin·ny (hwin′ē) *verb.* to make the low neighing sound that a horse makes. **whinnied.**

wig·gle (wig″l) *verb.* to twist or turn quickly from side to side. **wiggled.**

wor·ship (wʉr′ship) *noun.* **1.** a church service; prayer. **2.** great love or admiration of any kind. —*verb.* **1.** to offer prayers; attend church. **2.** to show great love or admiration.

worst (wʉrst) *adjective.* the most bad, harmful, etc.; least good.

wor·thy (wʉr′thē) *adjective.* **1.** having value or being wanted. **2.** being good enough for something.

writ·er (rīt′ər) *noun.* someone who writes books, essays, poems, etc., especially as a way to earn a living; author.

Y

yeowled (yould) *verb.* to yell or howl; give a loud howling cry.

yowl (youl) *verb.* to howl or cry out in a long, sad way.

a	fat	oi	oil	ch	chin
ā	ape	oo	look	sh	she
ä	car, father	ōo	tool	th	thin
e	ten	ou	out	th	then
er	care	u	up	zh	leisure
ē	even	ur	fur	ṅg	ring
i	hit				
ir	here	ə =	a *in* ago		
ī	bite, fire		e *in* agent		
o	lot		i *in* unity		
ō	go		o *in* collect		
ô	law, horn		u *in* focus		

wasp

weather vane

The authors listed below have written some of the selections that appear in this book. The content of the notes was determined by a survey of what readers wanted to know about authors.

EDWARD ARDIZZONE

EDWARD ARDIZZONE

Edward Ardizzone was born in Haiphong, Indochina, in what is today the country of Vietnam. When he was five years old, he moved to England with his mother and sisters. He lived in England the rest of his life. There, Edward Ardizzone became a writer and illustrator. He once described how his children's pleas for stories led him to create his books and illustrations. They would ask, "Daddy, please, please tell us a story" or "Daddy, please, draw us a picture of two elephants having a fight." It was in this way that the stories were created. Edward Ardizzone won many awards for his books, including the Kate Greenaway Medal for *Tim All Alone. (1900–1979)*

GWENDOLYN BROOKS

The poet Gwendolyn Brooks was born in
Topeka, Kansas. She says, "I loved poetry very
early and began to put rhymes together at about
seven. At the age of thirteen, my poem 'Eventide'
was accepted and printed in a children's magazine."
When she was sixteen, she began submitting poems
to a newspaper, and more than 75 of them were
published. Gwendolyn Brooks won the Pulitzer
Prize in poetry in 1950 for "Annie Allen."
(Born 1917)

GWENDOLYN BROOKS

ANN CAMERON

From the time Ann Cameron was in the third
grade, she knew she wanted to be a writer. She says
that her desire to be a writer came from her love
of books. She says, "A book is something like a
message in a bottle that an author throws out to sea;
you never know whom it might reach, or how much
it might mean to them." Ann Cameron believes that
writers should write the stories they want to write:
"Your story, if it's really the way you want to tell it,
can never be wrong the way an arithmetic answer is
wrong; and even if your mother, your father, your
teacher, or your best friend doesn't understand it,
it's still right for you." *(Born 1943)*

ANN CAMERON

LEWIS CARROLL

LEWIS CARROLL

Lewis Carroll's real name was Charles Lutwidge Dodgson. He taught mathematics in England, but he is best known for his book *Alice's Adventures in Wonderland.* He made up the stories about Alice to tell to the children of a friend. The girls liked the stories so much they asked him to write them down. Later, he wrote another book about Alice. It is called *Through the Looking Glass. (1832–1898)*

LYDIA MARIA CHILD

LYDIA MARIA CHILD

Lydia Maria Child was born in Medford, Massachusetts. She was the youngest of six children. Her father was a baker. He made "Medford Crackers," which were very popular. He was able to give all his children a good education. Lydia Maria Child started the first U.S. magazine for children. She also wrote novels, books of games for children, and many articles against slavery. *(1802–1880)*

RAY CRUZ

Ray Cruz was born in New York City and still lives there. He studied at the High School of Art and Design, at Pratt Institute, and at Cooper Union. He has designed textiles and wallpapers and packaging for cosmetic firms. He has illustrated books for ten publishers. Ray Cruz says that he is now engaged in a personal project to illustrate a group of fairy tales in full color. *(Born 1933)*

RACHEL FIELD

Rachel Field's book *Hitty: Her First Hundred Years* won the Newbery Medal. She was the first woman to win this award. Rachel Field said she spent time writing before she did much reading. "It wasn't that I could not have read earlier. I knew the letters and all that, but it was so much more pleasant to have my mother read books to me." *(1894–1942)*

RACHEL FIELD

PAUL GALDONE

Paul Galdone is an author and illustrator of books for young people. He was born in Budapest, Hungary. He and his family moved to the United States in 1928. He had a difficult time in school because he did not speak English well. He liked biology class, however, because he could draw grasshoppers. "I was soon drawing them for all the other pupils." He has won awards for his books. He has twice been the runner-up for the Caldecott Medal. *(Born 1914)*

PAUL GALDONE

HELEN V. GRIFFITH

Helen V. Griffith says, "I have been writing and drawing since I could handle a pencil. When I was very young I wrote poetry, usually about animals. I have always liked animals, and a dog has had a featured role in many books I've written. I don't begin by thinking, 'I'm going to write about a dog,' but that's what happens." *(Born 1934)*

HELEN V. GRIFFITH

MALCOLM HALL

MALCOLM HALL

Malcolm Hall was born in Chicago, Illinois, but he grew up in Los Alamos, New Mexico. He says that the town of Los Alamos is a bit strange, because "the town itself is located on a 7000-foot mesa in the Sangre de Cristo Mountains." Both Malcolm Hall's mother and father were physicists. Malcolm Hall has written over 30 filmstrips. His book *Headlines* was a Junior Literary Guild selection. *(Born 1945)*

LEE BENNETT HOPKINS

LEE BENNETT HOPKINS

Lee Bennett Hopkins has interviewed, or talked with, many writers and illustrators. He writes about his talks with these people. He also writes poems for young people. He says, "I love doing children's books. Each one is a new challenge, a new day, a new spring for me." Lee Bennett Hopkins also puts together anthologies, or collections, of other people's poems. He goes through thousands of poems and chooses the twenty that he thinks children will enjoy most. *(Born 1938)*

JOHANNA HURWITZ

Johanna Hurwitz is a writer and illustrator of
books for young people. She is also a children's
librarian. She says, "My parents met in a bookstore
and there has never been a moment when books
were not important in my life." Johanna Hurwitz
writes many letters to friends and relatives. She
thinks the letter writing she does is very good
training for her book writing. Her husband is also
a writer. She thinks that her two children will
probably be writers, too. "After all," she says,
"what do you expect? Their grandparents met in
a bookstore." *(Born 1937)*

JOHANNA HURWITZ

RACHEL ISADORA

Rachel Isadora writes and illustrates children's
books. She is also a ballet dancer. She has been
dancing since she was eleven years old. Rachel
Isadora is an award-winning author. One of the
awards she has won is the Boston Globe–Horn
Book Award for her book *Ben's Trumpet*. Rachel
Isadora's husband also writes books for young
people. She has illustrated some of her husband's
books, too.

RACHEL ISADORA

Genie Iverson

GENIE IVERSON

Genie Iverson was born in Newport News, Virginia, where her father was an officer in the Navy. She has been a reporter on a newspaper. Now she writes fables for young people as well as nonfiction. She says she writes biographies because she is interested in people and in history.
(Born 1942)

Ada B. Litchfield

ADA B. LITCHFIELD

Ada B. Litchfield grew up on Cape Cod, Massachusetts. She began writing when she was a little girl. She has published many TV scripts and books. Her TV script *Up Close and Natural* won the Ohio State Merit Award in the Natural and Physical Science Category. Ada B. Litchfield and her husband live in Stoughton, Massachusetts, with their cat Lit'l One.

PHYLLIS MCGINLEY

Phyllis McGinley wrote stories and poems for children and for adults. The first children's book she wrote was *The Horse Who Lived Upstairs*. When Phyllis McGinley wrote that book, she lived in New York City. She went to Greenwich Village to see how city horses lived. She said, "I discovered one stable that cried out for story-telling. The horses all were kept on the upper floors of the building, and they surveyed the world from their second-story windows as calmly as though they were standing in country pastures. When I noticed that their watering trough was an old cast-off bathtub, I knew I had a book." She won awards for both her poems and her stories. *(1905–1978)*

PHYLLIS MCGINLEY

EVE MERRIAM

Eve Merriam has written many poems for both children and adults. She has also written books, plays, and stories. "I was writing poems when I was about seven or eight. One of my first was about a birch tree that grew outside my bedroom window. It never occurred to me that someday I might like to be a writer. I just wrote. I think one is chosen to be a poet. You write poems because you must write them; because you can't live your life without writing them." Her advice to young people who want to be writers is, "Don't be discouraged." *(Born 1916)*

EVE MERRIAM

A. A. MILNE

A. A. MILNE

Alan Alexander Milne wrote many stories and poems for children. Milne first began writing when he was seventeen. He said, "It was in the Christmas holidays of 1899 that I discovered the itch for writing which has never quite left me." He started out by writing poems. Later he began writing stories. Some of his stories are about a boy named Christopher Robin and a bear named Winnie-the-Pooh. Milne's only son was also named Christopher Robin. *(1882–1956)*

LILIAN MOORE

LILIAN MOORE

Lilian Moore was born in New York City. She writes books and poetry for young people. She has also been a schoolteacher. She taught children who had been out of school. They did not know how to read. Lilian Moore said that she was annoyed because she could not find interesting books for these children to read, so she decided to write her own books for them. She has written more than forty books since then. Some of Lilian Moore's books have been chosen as American Library Association Notable Books.

E. H. SHEPARD

E. H. SHEPARD

Ernest Howard Shepard was born in England where he lived all his life. He said that he had always intended to be an artist of some kind. Both his father and mother encouraged him in his art. He drew cartoons for the famous English magazine *Punch* for nearly fifty years. He also illustrated many books. Among the books he illustrated are *The Wind in the Willows*, *The Reluctant Dragon*, and *The Secret Garden*. He is probably best known for having illustrated the Christopher Robin books by A. A. Milne. He had two children. His son was killed in World War II. His daughter illustrated the Mary Poppins books. In 1972, E. H. Shepard was the recipient of the Order of the British Empire in recognition of his artistic works. *(1879–1976)*

ELIZABETH SHUB

ELIZABETH SHUB

Elizabeth Shub was born in Poland. She came to the United States when she was a child. She writes books for children and also translates books into English for other writers. She helped Isaac Bashevis Singer translate *Zlateh the Goat, and Other Stories* from Yiddish. One of her books is *Seeing Is Believing*.

JOHN STEPTOE

JOHN STEPTOE

John Steptoe was a painter and a writer and also taught at the Brooklyn Music School. He illustrated all of his own books as well as books for other writers. He received the Gold Medal from the Society of Illustrators for the book *Stevie*. He wrote that book when he was only sixteen years old. He said that one of the reasons he began writing books for young people was the need for "books that black children could honestly relate to." John Steptoe's new book, *Mufaro's Beautiful Daughters,* was named a Caldecott Honor Book and won the 1987 Boston Globe–Horn Book Award. *(1950–1989)*

JAMES STEVENSON

JAMES STEVENSON

James Stevenson is a writer and illustrator. Although he began his career as a cartoonist and artist, he always wanted to be a writer. He wrote magazine articles and books for adults before he began writing children's books. Now, he has written many books for young people. Several of his books have been chosen as Junior Literary Guild selections and American Library Association Notable Books. *(Born 1929)*

BRINTON TURKLE

Brinton Turkle has written and illustrated several books for children. He illustrates books for other authors, too. Brinton Turkle believes that, in a picture book, the words and the pictures should be so closely related to each other that neither one "can stand successfully alone." He says, "I feel that I have had only marginal success with this ideal, but I do keep trying and I think I am getting better." *(Born 1915)*

BRINTON TURKLE

YOSHIKO UCHIDA

Yoshiko Uchida's last name is pronounced ō chē′də. She writes books about Japan and its people and about Japanese-Americans as well. She says, "I wanted American children to become familiar with the marvelous Japanese folk tales I had heard in my childhood. I wanted them to read about Japanese children, learning to understand and respect differences in customs and culture, but realizing also that basically human beings are alike the world over, with similar joys and hopes." Some of Yoshiko Uchida's books have been selected as American Library Association Notable Books. She has also illustrated some of her own books of Japanese folk tales. *(Born 1921)*

YOSHIKO UCHIDA

JUDITH VIORST

JUDITH VIORST

Judith Viorst began writing poetry when she was seven years old. She says she wrote "terrible poems about dead dogs, mostly." She did not become a successful writer until she was grown and began writing about her own family. Now she is an award-winning author. Judith Viorst says, "Most of my children's books are for or about my own children." *(Born 1931)*

BERNARD WABER

BERNARD WABER

Bernard Waber is an author and illustrator. He has written several books about Lyle the Crocodile. Since he started writing the Lyle books, his house has become almost like a museum of crocodile things. He says there are stuffed toy crocodiles on "tables, sofas, stairs, floors, or whatever surface is available. A claw-footed bathtub—identical to the one shared at the Primm household—sits in our foyer together with its stuffed, Lyle-type occupant." Bernard Waber has won several awards for his books, including the Lewis Carroll Shelf Award.

LEONARD WEISGARD

Leonard Weisgard writes and illustrates children's books. He has won many awards for his books, including the Caldecott Medal. He says about his work, "My art studies were of value to me, but I also learned how to illustrate books by learning to dance, living, breathing, being with children, with people, being alone, reading, writing, traveling, brooding, dreaming, beachcombing, wondering, and mostly, listening to Margaret Wise Brown." He believes that an artist can find art materials in everyday things: "There is the world to choose from—clothes, bobby or cotter pins, paper clips, metal hangers, ironing boards, baking pans, and cupcake tins. Put them all together and you have an artist's studio." *(Born 1916)*

LEONARD WEISGARD

AUTHOR INDEX

BOOKS TO ENJOY

Page 99: Jacket art from *And Then What Happened, Paul Revere?* by Jean Fritz, pictures by Margot Tomes. Illustrations copyright © 1973 by Margot Tomes. Reprinted by permission of Coward, McCann & Geoghegan, Inc., a division of The Putnam Publishing Group.

Page 99: Jacket art reproduced with permission of Charles Scribner's Sons, an imprint of Macmillan Publishing Company from *The Bears on Hemlock Mountain* by Alice Dalgliesh, illustrated by Helen Sewell. Copyright 1952 Alice Dalgliesch; copyright renewed.

Page 99: Jacket art from *The Farm Book* by E. Boyd Smith, copyright 1910 by the Fairfield County Council, Boy Scouts of America, copyright renewed 1938. Reprinted by permission of Houghton Mifflin Company.

Page 99: Jacket art from *Wagon Wheels* by Barbara Brenner, pictures by Don Bolognese. Illustrations copyright © 1978 by Don Bolognese. Reprinted by permission of Harper & Row, Publishers, Inc.

Page 181: Jacket art from *Amy Goes Fishing* by Jean Marzollo, pictures by Ann Schweninger. Pictures copyright © by Ann Schweninger. Reproduced by permission of the American publisher, Dial Books for Young Readers, and of the British publisher, The Bodley Head Ltd.

Page 181: Jacket art reproduced by permission of Walker and Company from *A First Look at Seashells* by Millicent E. Selsam and Joyce Hunt, illustrated by Harriet Springer. Illustrations copyright © 1983 by Harriet Springer. Reprinted by permission of Walker Publishing Company, Inc.

Page 181: Jacket art reproduced with permission of Four Winds Press, an Imprint of Macmillan Publishing Company from *Little Whale* by Ann McGovern, illustrated by John Hamburger. Illustration Copyright © 1979 by John Hamburger.

Page 181: Jacket art from *Sea Songs* by Myra Cohn Livingston, paintings by Leonard Everett Fisher. Illustrations copyright © 1986 by Leonard Everett Fisher. Reprinted by permission of Holiday House Inc.

Page 249: Jacket art reproduced with permission of Charles Scribner's Sons, an imprint of Macmillan Publishing Company from *The Courage of Sarah Noble* by Alice Dalgliesh, illustrated by Leonard Weisgard. Copyright 1954 Alice Dalgliesh and Leonard Weisgard; copyright renewed.

Page 249: Jacket art from *Anna, Grandpa, and the Big Storm* by Carla Stevens, pictures by Margot Tomes. Illustrations copyright © 1982 by Margot Tomes. Reprinted by permission of Houghton Mifflin Company.

Page 249: Jacket art reproduced with permission of the American publisher, Margaret K. McElderry Books, an imprint of Macmillan Publishing Company, and of the Canadian publisher, Douglas & McIntyre, from *Chin Chiang and the Dragon's Dance* by Ian Wallace. Copyright © 1984 Ian Wallace.

Page 345: Jacket art from *Train Whistles: A Language in Code* by Helen Roney Sattler, illustrated by Tom Funk. Reprinted by permission of Lothrop, Lee & Shepard, a division of William Morrow & Company, Inc.

Page 345: Jacket art from *Computers* by Jane Jonas Srivastava, illustrated by James and Ruth McCrea reprinted by permission of Thomas Y. Crowell, an imprint of Harper & Row, Publishers Inc.

Page 345: Jacket art from *The Seeing Stick* by Jane Yolen, pictures by Remy Charlip and Demetra Maraslis. Illustrations copyright © 1977 by Remy Charlip and Demetra Maraslis. Reprinted by permission of Thomas Y. Crowell, an imprint of Harper & Row, Publishers, Inc.

Page 345: Jacket art from *Finger Rhymes* collected and illustrated by Marc Brown. Copyright © 1980 by Marc Brown. Reproduced by permission of the publisher, E. P. Dutton, a division of NAL Penguin Inc.

TIME OUT FOR BOOKS

Art from *The Nightingale* translated by Eva Le Gallienne, illustrated by Nancy Ekholm Burkert. Pictures copyright © 1965 by Nancy Ekholm Burkert. Reprinted by permission of the American publisher, Harper & Row, Publishers, Inc., and of illustrator's British agents, Sinnott & Associates.

Art from *Storm in the Night* by Mary Stolz, illustrated by Pat Cummings. Illustrations copyright © 1988 by Pat Cummings. Reprinted by permission of Harper & Row, Publishers, Inc.

LITERATURE LINKS

Page 142: "Whales Are Mammals" from *Whales*, created and written by John Bonnett Wexo, copyright © 1983 John Bonnett Wexo. Published by Wildlife Education, Ltd.

Page 286: Peanuts cartoon by Charles Schulz reprinted by permission of United Feature Syndicate, Inc.

Page 311: Excerpt from "The Musicians of Bremen Town" adapted from Grimms' Fairy Tales by Walter Roberts from *Plays from Favorite Folk Tales* edited by Sylvia E. Kamerman, published by Plays, Inc.

COVER: Loretta Lustig
DESIGN: Design Five, NYC and Kirchoff/ Wohlberg in cooperation with Silver Burdett & Ginn

ILLUSTRATION: 4, (tl) Brinton Turkle, (tr) James Stevenson, (bl) James Stevenson; 5, (tr) James Stevenson, (bl) Roni Shephero, (br) Rachel Isadora; 6, (t) Scott Pollack, (c) Edward Ardizzone, (bl) Bernard Waber, (br) Linda Shute; 7, (tr) Paul Galdone, (cl) Edward Ardizzone; 8, (t) Ray Criz, (br) Troy Howell; 9, (bl) Rae Ecklund, (br) Troy Howell; 10, (tl) E. H. Shepard, (tr) Bruce Degen, (b) E. H. Shepard; 11, (bl) Ashley Wolff, (bc) Bruce Degen, (br) Lane Gregory; 14–22, James Stevenson; 24–25, Wendy Edelson; 28–36, Brinton Turkle; 56–68, James Stevenson; 70–71, Andrea Eberbach; 72– 80, Rachel Isadora; 82–83, Tony Chen; 84–95, Leonard Weisgard; 84, Betsy Day; 98, Susan Jaekel; 102–114, Edward Ardizzone; 118, Edward Ardizzone; 119, Linda Shute; 120–130, Linda Shute; 134–135, Gary Torrisi; 137, Gary Torrisi; 141, Susan Jaekel; 150–158, Paul Galdone; 159, Sharron O'Neil; 160–161, Scott Pollack; 163, Susan Banta; 164–177, Bernard Waber; 180, Sharron O'Neil; 193, Susan Lexa; 196–204, Rae Ecklund; 206, Floyd Cooper; 211, Christa Kieffer; 212–213, Rae Ecklund; 236–237, Pat Cummings, Troy Howell; 214–224, Ann Strugnell; 233, Susan Jaekel; 238–245, Ray Cruz; 248, Sharron O'Neil; 252–262, Bruce Degen; 252, Bob Filipowich; 263, Sharron O'Neil; 264–265, Greg Mackey; 266–275, Larry Raymond; 276–277, (b & tr) Rich Lo; 280–281, Lane Gregory; 286, Charles Schultz; 288–294, Les Morrill; 295, Sharron O'Neil; 296–308, John Steptoe; 311, Ashley Wolff; 312–322, Ashley Wolff; 323, Sharron O'Neil; 324–341, E. H. Shephard; 344, Susan Jaekel; 347, Diane Dawson Hearn, Claudia Sargent; 348, Roberta Holmes; 351, Deirdre Griffin; 353, Roberta Holmes; 355, Diane Dawson Hearn; 356, Deirdre Griffin, Diane Dawson Hearn; 357, Deirdre Griffin; 358, Roberta Holmes; 359, Claudia Sargent; 360, Diane Dawson Hearn; 361, Melinda Fabian; 362, Diane Dawson Hearn, Claudia Sargent; 363, Claudia Sargent; 364, Diane Dawson Hearn, Roberta Holmes.

PHOTOGRAPHY: 7, Jen & Des Bartlett/Bruce Coleman, Inc.; 8, Laird Roberts; 12, *Snap the Whip*, Winslow Homer (American), 50.41, The Metropolitan Museum of Art, New York; 39, The Pilgrim Society, Plymouth; 40, Bettmann Archive; 41, The Pilgrim Society, Plymouth; 42, courtesy The John Hancock Mutual Life Insurance Co., Boston; 43, The Granger Collection; 100, © Susan Van Etten; 116–117, Superstock; 133, Woods Hole Oceanographic Institute, Courtesy Sygma; 135, RONA/Bruce Coleman, Inc.; 136, Woods Hole Oceanographic Institute; 139– 140, Woods Hole Oceanographic Institute; 142, Steven Gottlieb/FPG International; 143, Jeff Foott/Bruce Coleman, Inc.; 144, Jeff Foott/Bruce Coleman, Inc.; 145, Jen & Des Bartlett/Bruce Coleman, Inc.; 146, G. L. Kooyman/Animals, Animals; 147, Jeff Foott/Tom Stack & Associates; 148, Rod Allin/Tom Stack & Associates; 162, Bettmann Archive; 182, Boy *Juggling Shell*, Hokusai (Japanese), 14.76.59.4, The Metropolitan Museum of Art, New York; 185–190, Laird Roberts; 191, Mary Anne Facelman-Miner, The White House; 192, Laird Roberts; 206, Eduardo Patino; 209, Eduardo Patino; 226, The Granger Collection; 228, Thomas Bewick, Dover Books; 229, The Granger Collection; 231, National Portrait Gallery, Smithsonian Institution; 250, *The Letter*, 1871, Mary Cassatt, American 1844–1926, gift of The William Emerson and Charles Henry Hayden Fund, 41.803, 10.84, Museum of Fine Arts, Boston; 276, Carlos Vergara; 277, (tl) North Wind Picture Archives; 278–279, Dan Helms/Duomo; 282, Steven Goldstein, Courtesy St. Louis Cardinals; 283, Focus on Sports; 310, Miro Vintoniv/Picture Cube; 348, Sera Hopkins; 349, Stephen G. Maka; 350, Stephen G. Maka; 351, Leon Poindexter; 354, Carla Palau, © Frank Siteman 1988; 355, © Frank Siteman 1988; Dante Gelmetti/Bruce Coleman, Inc.; 358, Nicholas de Vore III/Bruce Coleman, Inc.; 360, © Frank Siteman 1988; 361, Mike Mazzaschi/ Stock Boston; 365, C. W. Perkins/Animals, Animals; 366, Bettmann Archive/BBC Hulton; 367, (t) *Los Angeles Times*, (b) Fernando Diaz Rivera; 368, (t & b) Bettmann Archive; 369, (t) Bettmann Archive, (c) Clarion, (b) Holiday House; 370, (t) provided by author, (b) Antique Images/Putnam; 371, (t) Viking Penguin; 373, (t) The Granger Collection; 374, (t) Bettmann Archive; 376 (b) Edward E. Davis; 377, (t) Dial Dutton, Viking Penguin, (b) McElderry Books; 378, (t) Milton Viorst, (b) H. W. Wilson Co.; 379, Western Publishing.

B C D E F G H I J — RRD — 96 95 94 93 92 91 90